RUS

PLATO

Translated by
BENJAMIN JOWETT

INTRODUCTION

The Phaedrus is closely connected with the Symposium, and may be regarded either as introducing or following it. The two Dialogues together contain the whole philosophy of Plato on the nature of love, which in the Republic and in the later writings of Plato is only introduced playfully or as a figure of speech. But in the Phaedrus and Symposium love and philosophy join hands, and one is an aspect of the other. The spiritual and emotional part is elevated into the ideal, to which in the Symposium mankind are described as looking forward, and which in the Phaedrus, as well as in the Phaedo, they are seeking to recover from a former state of existence. Whether the subject of the Dialogue is love or rhetoric, or the union of the two, or the relation of philosophy to love and to art in general, and to the human soul, will be hereafter considered. And perhaps we may arrive at some conclusion such as the following—that the dialogue is not strictly confined to a single subject, but passes from one to another with the natural freedom of conversation.

Phaedrus has been spending the morning with Lysias, the celebrated rhetorician, and is going to refresh himself by taking a walk outside the wall, when he is met by Socrates, who professes that he will not leave him until he has delivered up the speech with which Lysias has regaled him, and which he is carrying about in his mind, or more probably in a book hidden under his cloak, and is intending to study as he walks. The imputation is not denied, and the two agree to direct their steps out of the public way along the stream of the Ilissus towards a plane-tree which is seen in the distance. There, lying down amidst pleasant sounds and scents, they will read the speech of Lysias. The country is a novelty to Socrates, who never goes out of the town; and hence he is full of admiration for the beauties of nature, which he seems to be drinking in for the first time.

As they are on their way, Phaedrus asks the opinion of Socrates respecting the local tradition of Boreas and Oreithyia. Socrates, after a satirical allusion to the 'rationalizers' of his day, replies that he has no time for these 'nice' interpretations of mythology, and he pities anyone who has. When you once begin there is no end of them, and they spring from an uncritical philosophy after all. 'The proper study of mankind is man;' and he is a far more complex and wonderful being than the serpent Typho. Socrates as yet does not know himself; and why should he care to know about unearthly monsters? Engaged in such conversation, they arrive at the plane-tree; when they have found a convenient resting-place, Phaedrus pulls out the speech and reads:—

The speech consists of a foolish paradox which is to the effect that the non-lover ought to be accepted rather than the lover— because he is more rational, more agreeable, more enduring, less suspicious, less hurtful, less boastful, less engrossing, and because there are more of them, and for a great many other reasons which are equally unmeaning. Phaedrus is captivated with the beauty of the periods, and wants to make Socrates say that nothing was or ever could be written better. Socrates does not think much of the matter, but then he has only attended to the form, and in that he has detected several repetitions and other marks of haste. He cannot agree with Phaedrus in the extreme value which he sets upon this performance, because he is afraid of doing injustice to

Anacreon and Sappho and other great writers, and is almost inclined to think that he himself, or rather some power residing within him, could make a speech better than that of Lysias on the same theme, and also different from his, if he may be allowed the use of a few commonplaces which all speakers must equally employ.

Phaedrus is delighted at the prospect of having another speech, and promises that he will set up a golden statue of Socrates at Delphi, if he keeps his word. Some raillery ensues, and at length Socrates, conquered by the threat that he shall never again hear a speech of Lysias unless he fulfils his promise, veils his face and begins.

First, invoking the Muses and assuming ironically the person of the non-lover (who is a lover all the same), he will enquire into the nature and power of love. For this is a necessary preliminary to the other question—How is the non-lover to be distinguished from the lover? In all of us there are two principles—a better and a worse—reason and desire, which are generally at war with one another; and the victory of the rational is called temperance, and the victory of the irrational intemperance or excess. The latter takes many forms and has many bad names—gluttony, drunkenness, and the like. But of all the irrational desires or excesses the greatest is that which is led away by desires of a kindred nature to the enjoyment of personal beauty. And this is the master power of love.

Here Socrates fancies that he detects in himself an unusual flow of eloquence—this newly-found gift he can only attribute to the inspiration of the place, which appears to be dedicated to the nymphs. Starting again from the philosophical basis which has been laid down, he proceeds to show how many advantages the non-lover has over the lover. The one encourages softness and effeminacy and exclusiveness; he cannot endure any superiority in his beloved; he will train him in luxury, he will keep him out of society, he will deprive him of parents, friends, money, knowledge, and of every other good, that he may have him all to himself. Then again his ways are not ways of pleasantness; he is mighty disagreeable; 'crabbed age and youth cannot live together.' At every hour of the night and day he is intruding upon him; there is the same old withered face and the remainder to match—and he is always repeating, in season or out of season, the praises or dispraises of his beloved, which are bad enough when he is sober, and published all over the world when he is drunk. At length his love ceases; he is converted into an enemy, and the spectacle may be seen of the lover running away from the beloved, who pursues him with vain reproaches, and demands his reward which the other refuses to pay. Too late the beloved learns, after all his pains and disagreeables, that 'As wolves love lambs so lovers love their loves.' (Compare Char.) Here is the end; the 'other' or 'non-lover' part of the speech had better be understood, for if in the censure of the lover Socrates has broken out in verse, what will he not do in his praise of the non-lover? He has said his say and is preparing to go away.

Phaedrus begs him to remain, at any rate until the heat of noon has passed; he would like to have a little more conversation before they go. Socrates, who has risen, recognizes the oracular sign which forbids him to depart until he has done penance. His conscious has been awakened, and like Stesichorus when he had reviled the lovely Helen he will sing a palinode for having blasphemed the majesty of love. His palinode takes the form of a myth.

Socrates begins his tale with a glorification of madness, which he divides into four kinds: first, there is the art of divination or prophecy—this, in a vein similar to that pervading the Cratylus and Io, he connects with madness by an etymological explanation (mantike, manike—compare oionoistike, oionistike, ''tis all one reckoning, save the phrase is a little variations'); secondly, there is the art of purification by mysteries; thirdly, poetry or the inspiration of the Muses (compare Ion), without which no man can enter their temple. All this shows that madness is one of heaven's blessings, and may sometimes be a great deal better than sense. There is also a fourth kind of madness—that of love—which cannot be explained without enquiring into the nature of the soul.

All soul is immortal, for she is the source of all motion both in herself and in others. Her form may be described in a figure as a composite nature made up of a charioteer and a pair of winged steeds. The steeds of the gods are immortal, but ours are one mortal and the other immortal. The immortal soul soars upwards into the heavens, but the mortal drops her plumes and settles upon the earth.

Now the use of the wing is to rise and carry the downward element into the upper world—there to behold beauty, wisdom, goodness, and the other things of God by which the soul is nourished. On a certain day Zeus the lord of heaven goes forth in a winged chariot; and an array of gods and demi-gods and of human souls in their train, follows him. There are glorious and blessed sights in the interior of heaven, and he who will may freely behold them. The great vision of all is seen at the feast of the gods, when they ascend the heights of the empyrean—all but Hestia, who is left at home to keep house. The chariots of the gods glide readily upwards and stand upon the outside; the revolution of the spheres carries them round, and they have a vision of the world beyond. But the others labour in vain; for the mortal steed, if he has not been properly trained, keeps them down and sinks them towards the earth. Of the world which is beyond the heavens, who can tell? There is an essence formless, colourless, intangible, perceived by the mind only, dwelling in the region of true knowledge. The divine mind in her revolution enjoys this fair prospect, and beholds justice, temperance, and knowledge in their everlasting essence. When fulfilled with the sight of them she returns home, and the charioteer puts up the horses in their stable, and gives them ambrosia to eat and nectar to drink. This is the life of the gods; the human soul tries to reach the same heights, but hardly succeeds; and sometimes the head of the charioteer rises above, and sometimes sinks below, the fair vision, and he is at last obliged, after much contention, to turn away and leave the plain of truth. But if the soul has followed in the train of her god and once beheld truth she is preserved from harm, and is carried round in the next revolution of the spheres; and if always following, and always seeing the truth, is then for ever unharmed. If, however, she drops her wings and falls to the earth, then she takes the form of man, and the soul which has seen most of the truth passes into a philosopher or lover; that which has seen truth in the second degree, into a king or warrior; the third, into a householder or money-maker; the fourth, into a gymnast; the fifth, into a prophet or mystic; the sixth, into a poet or imitator; the seventh, into a husbandman or craftsman; the eighth, into a sophist or demagogue; the ninth, into a tyrant. All these are states of probation, wherein he who lives righteously is improved, and he who lives unrighteously deteriorates. After death comes the judgment; the bad depart to houses of correction under the earth, the good to places of joy in heaven. When a thousand years have elapsed the souls meet together and choose the lives which they will lead for another period of existence. The soul which three times in succession has chosen the life of a philosopher or of a lover who is not without philosophy receives her wings at the close of the third millennium; the remainder have to complete a cycle of ten thousand years before their wings are restored to them. Each time there is full liberty of choice. The soul of a man may descend into a beast, and return again into the form of man. But the form of man will only be taken by the soul which has once seen truth and acquired some conception of the universal:—this is the recollection of the knowledge which she attained when in the company of the Gods. And men in general recall only with difficulty the things of another world, but the mind of the philosopher has a better remembrance of them. For when he beholds the visible beauty of earth his enraptured soul passes in thought to those glorious sights of justice and wisdom and temperance and truth which she once gazed upon in heaven. Then she celebrated holy mysteries and beheld blessed apparitions shining in pure light, herself pure, and not as yet entombed in the body. And still, like a bird eager to quit its cage, she flutters and looks upwards, and is therefore deemed mad. Such a recollection of past days she receives through sight, the keenest of our senses, because beauty, alone of the ideas, has any representation on earth: wisdom is invisible to mortal eyes. But the corrupted nature, blindly excited by this vision of beauty, rushes on to enjoy, and would fain wallow like a brute beast in sensual pleasures. Whereas the true mystic, who has seen the many sights of bliss, when he beholds a god-like form or face is amazed with delight, and if he were not afraid of being thought mad he would fall down and worship. Then the stiffened wing begins to relax and grow again; desire which has been imprisoned pours over the soul of the lover; the germ of the wing unfolds, and stings, and pangs of birth, like the cutting of teeth, are everywhere felt. (Compare Symp.) Father and mother, and goods and laws and proprieties are nothing to him; his beloved is his physician, who can alone cure his pain. An apocryphal sacred writer says that the power which thus works in him is by mortals called love, but the immortals call him dove, or the winged one, in order to represent the force of his wings—such at any rate is his nature. Now the characters of lovers depend upon the god whom they followed in the other world; and they choose their loves in this world accordingly. The followers of Ares are fierce and violent; those of Zeus seek out some philosophical and imperial nature; the attendants of Here find a royal love; and in like manner the followers of every god seek a love who is like their god; and to him they communicate the nature which they have received from their god. The manner in which they take their love is as follows:—

I told you about the charioteer and his two steeds, the one a noble animal who is guided by word and admonition only, the other an ill-looking villain who will hardly yield to blow or spur. Together all three, who are a figure of the soul, approach the vision of love. And now a fierce conflict begins. The ill-conditioned steed rushes on to enjoy, but the charioteer, who beholds the beloved with awe, falls back in adoration, and forces both the steeds on their haunches; again the evil steed rushes forwards and pulls shamelessly. The conflict grows more and more severe; and at last the charioteer, throwing himself backwards, forces the bit out of the clenched teeth of the brute, and pulling harder than ever at the reins, covers his tongue and jaws with blood, and forces him to rest his legs and haunches with pain upon the ground. When this has happened several times, the villain is tamed and humbled, and from that time forward the soul of the lover follows the beloved in modesty and holy fear. And now their bliss is consummated; the same image of love dwells in the breast of either, and if they have self-control, they pass their lives in the greatest happiness which is attainable by man—they continue masters of themselves, and conquer in one of the three heavenly victories. But if they choose the lower life of ambition they may still have a happy destiny, though inferior, because they have not the approval of the whole soul. At last they leave the body and proceed on their pilgrim's progress, and those who have once begun can never go back. When the time comes they receive their wings and fly away, and the lovers have the same wings.

Socrates concludes:—

These are the blessings of love, and thus have I made my recantation in finer language than before: I did so in order to please Phaedrus. If I said what was wrong at first, please to attribute my error to Lysias, who ought to study philosophy instead of rhetoric, and then he will not mislead his disciple Phaedrus.

Phaedrus is afraid that he will lose conceit of Lysias, and that Lysias will be out of conceit with himself, and leave off making speeches, for the politicians have been deriding him. Socrates is of opinion that there is small danger of this; the politicians are themselves the great rhetoricians of the age, who desire to attain immortality by the authorship of laws. And therefore there is nothing with which they can reproach Lysias in being a writer; but there may be disgrace in being a bad one.

And what is good or bad writing or speaking? While the sun is hot in the sky above us, let us ask that question: since by rational conversation man lives, and not by the indulgence of bodily pleasures. And the grasshoppers who are chirruping around may carry our words to the Muses, who are their patronesses; for the grasshoppers were human beings themselves in a world before the Muses, and when the Muses came they died of hunger for the love of song. And they carry to them in heaven the report of those who honour them on earth.

The first rule of good speaking is to know and speak the truth; as a Spartan proverb says, 'true art is truth'; whereas rhetoric is an art of enchantment, which makes things appear good and evil, like and unlike, as the speaker pleases. Its use is not confined, as people commonly suppose, to arguments in the law courts and speeches in the assembly; it is rather a part of the art of disputation, under which are included both the rules of Gorgias and the eristic of Zeno. But it is not wholly devoid of truth. Superior knowledge enables us to deceive another by the help of resemblances, and to escape from such a deception when employed against ourselves. We see therefore that even in rhetoric an element of truth is required. For if we do not know the truth, we can neither make the gradual departures from truth by which men are most easily deceived, nor guard ourselves against deception.

Socrates then proposes that they shall use the two speeches as illustrations of the art of rhetoric; first distinguishing between the debatable and undisputed class of subjects. In the debatable class there ought to be a definition of all disputed matters. But there was no such definition in the speech of Lysias; nor is there any order or connection in his words any more than in a nursery rhyme. With this he compares the regular divisions of the other speech, which was his own (and yet not his own, for the local deities must have inspired him). Although only a playful composition, it will be found to embody two principles: first, that of synthesis or the comprehension of parts in a whole; secondly, analysis, or the resolution of the whole into parts. These are the processes of division and generalization which are so dear to the dialectician, that king of men. They are effected by dialectic, and not by rhetoric, of which the remains are but scanty after order and arrangement have been subtracted. There is nothing left but a heap of 'ologies' and other technical terms invented by Polus, Theodorus, Evenus, Tisias, Gorgias, and others, who have rules for everything, and who teach how to be short or long at pleasure. Prodicus showed his good sense when he said that there was a better thing than either to be short or long, which was to be of convenient length.

Still, notwithstanding the absurdities of Polus and others, rhetoric has great power in public assemblies. This power, however, is not given by any technical rules, but is the gift of genius. The real art is always being confused by rhetoricians with the preliminaries of the art. The perfection of oratory is like the perfection of anything else; natural power must be aided by art. But the art is not that which is taught in the schools of rhetoric; it is nearer akin to philosophy. Pericles, for instance, who was the most accomplished of all speakers, derived his eloquence not from rhetoric but from the philosophy of nature which he learnt of Anaxagoras. True rhetoric is like medicine, and the rhetorician has to consider the natures of men's souls as the physician considers the natures of their bodies. Such and such persons are to be affected in this way, such and such others in that; and he must know the times and the seasons for saying this or that. This is not an easy task, and this, if there be such an art, is the art of rhetoric.

I know that there are some professors of the art who maintain probability to be stronger than truth. But we maintain that probability is engendered by likeness of the truth which can only be attained by the knowledge of it, and that the aim of the good man should not be to please or persuade his fellow-servants, but to please his good masters who are the gods. Rhetoric has a fair beginning in this.

Enough of the art of speaking; let us now proceed to consider the true use of writing. There is an old Egyptian tale of Theuth, the inventor of writing, showing his invention to the god Thamus, who told him that he would only spoil men's memories and take away their understandings. From this tale, of which young Athens will probably make fun, may be gathered the lesson that writing is inferior to speech. For it is like a picture, which can give no answer to a question, and has only a deceitful likeness of a living creature. It has no power of adaptation, but uses the same words for all. It is not a legitimate son of knowledge, but a bastard, and when an attack is made upon this bastard neither parent nor anyone else is there to defend it. The husbandman will not seriously incline to sow his seed in such a hot-bed or garden of Adonis; he will rather sow in the natural soil of the human soul which has depth of earth; and he will anticipate the inner growth of the mind, by writing only, if at all, as a remedy against old age. The natural process will be far nobler, and will bring forth fruit in the minds of others as well as in his own.

The conclusion of the whole matter is just this,—that until a man knows the truth, and the manner of adapting the truth to the natures of other men, he cannot be a good orator; also, that the living is better than the written word, and that the principles of justice and truth when delivered by word of mouth are the legitimate offspring of a man's own bosom, and their lawful descendants take up their abode in others. Such an orator as he is who is possessed of them, you and I would fain become. And to all composers in the world, poets, orators, legislators, we hereby announce that if their compositions are based upon these principles, then they are not only poets, orators, legislators, but philosophers. All others are mere flatterers and putters together of words. This is the message which Phaedrus undertakes to carry to Lysias from the local deities, and Socrates himself will carry a similar message to his favourite Isocrates, whose future distinction as a great rhetorician he prophesies. The heat of the day has passed, and after offering up a prayer to Pan and the nymphs, Socrates and Phaedrus depart.

There are two principal controversies which have been raised about the Phaedrus; the first relates to the subject, the second to the date of the Dialogue.

There seems to be a notion that the work of a great artist like Plato cannot fail in unity, and that the unity of a dialogue requires a single subject. But the conception of unity really applies in very different degrees and ways to different kinds of art; to a statue, for example, far more than to any kind of literary composition, and to some species of literature far more than to others. Nor does the dialogue appear to be a style of composition in which the requirement of unity is most stringent; nor should the idea of unity derived from one sort of art be hastily transferred to another. The double titles of several of the Platonic Dialogues are a further proof that the severer rule was not observed by Plato. The Republic is divided between the search after justice and the construction of the ideal state; the Parmenides between the criticism of the Platonic ideas and of the Eleatic one or being; the Gorgias between the art of speaking and the nature of the good; the Sophist between the detection of the Sophist and the correlation of ideas. The Theaetetus, the Politicus, and the Philebus have also digressions which are but remotely connected with the main subject.

Thus the comparison of Plato's other writings, as well as the reason of the thing, lead us to the conclusion that we must not expect to find one idea pervading a whole work, but one, two, or more, as the invention of the writer may suggest, or his fancy wander. If each dialogue were confined to the development of a single idea, this would appear on the face of the dialogue, nor could any controversy be raised as to whether the Phaedrus treated of love or rhetoric. But the truth is that Plato subjects himself to no rule of this sort. Like every great artist he gives unity of form to the different and apparently distracting topics which he brings together. He works freely and is not to be supposed to have arranged every part of the dialogue before he begins to write. He fastens or weaves together the frame of his discourse loosely and imperfectly, and which is the warp and which is the woof cannot always be determined.

The subjects of the Phaedrus (exclusive of the short introductory passage about mythology which is suggested by the local tradition) are first the false or conventional art of rhetoric; secondly, love or the inspiration of beauty and knowledge, which is described as madness; thirdly, dialectic or the art of composition and division; fourthly, the true rhetoric, which is based upon dialectic, and is neither the art of persuasion nor knowledge of the truth alone, but the art of persuasion founded on knowledge of truth and knowledge of character; fifthly, the superiority of the spoken over the written word. The continuous thread which appears and reappears throughout is rhetoric; this is the ground into which the rest of the Dialogue is worked, in parts embroidered with fine words which are not in Socrates' manner, as he says, 'in order to please Phaedrus.' The speech of Lysias which has thrown Phaedrus into an ecstacy is adduced as an example of the false rhetoric; the first speech of Socrates, though an improvement, partakes of the same character; his second speech, which is full of that higher element said to have been learned of Anaxagoras by Pericles, and which in the midst of poetry does not forget order, is an illustration of the higher or true rhetoric. This higher rhetoric is based upon dialectic, and dialectic is a sort of inspiration akin to love (compare Symp.); in these two aspects of philosophy the technicalities of rhetoric are absorbed. And so the example becomes also the deeper theme of discourse. The true knowledge of things in heaven and earth is based upon enthusiasm or love of the ideas going before us and ever present to us in this world and in another; and the true order of speech or writing proceeds accordingly. Love, again, has three degrees: first, of interested love corresponding to the conventionalities of rhetoric; secondly, of disinterested or mad love, fixed on objects of sense, and answering, perhaps, to poetry; thirdly, of disinterested love directed towards the unseen, answering to dialectic or the science of the ideas. Lastly, the art of rhetoric in the lower sense is found to rest on a knowledge of the natures and characters of men, which Socrates at the commencement of the Dialogue has described as his own peculiar study.

Thus amid discord a harmony begins to appear; there are many links of connection which are not visible at first sight. At the same time the Phaedrus, although one of the most beautiful of the Platonic Dialogues, is also more irregular than any other. For insight into the world, for sustained irony, for depth of thought, there is no Dialogue superior, or perhaps equal to it. Nevertheless the form of the work has tended to obscure some of Plato's higher aims.

The first speech is composed 'in that balanced style in which the wise love to talk' (Symp.). The characteristics of rhetoric are insipidity, mannerism, and monotonous parallelism of clauses. There is more rhythm than reason; the creative power of imagination is wanting.

"Tis Greece, but living Greece no more.'

Plato has seized by anticipation the spirit which hung over Greek literature for a thousand years afterwards. Yet doubtless there were some who, like Phaedrus, felt a delight in the harmonious cadence and the pedantic reasoning of the rhetoricians newly imported from Sicily, which had ceased to be awakened in them by really great works, such as the odes of Anacreon or Sappho or the orations of Pericles. That the first speech was really written by Lysias is improbable. Like the poem of Solon, or the story of Thamus and Theuth, or the funeral oration of Aspasia (if genuine), or the pretence of Socrates in the Cratylus that his knowledge of philology is derived from Euthyphro, the invention is really due to the imagination of Plato, and may be compared to the parodies of the Sophists in the Protagoras. Numerous fictions of this sort occur in the Dialogues, and the gravity of Plato has sometimes imposed upon his commentators. The introduction of a considerable writing of another would seem not to be in keeping with a great work of art, and has no parallel elsewhere.

In the second speech Socrates is exhibited as beating the rhetoricians at their own weapons; he 'an unpractised man and they masters of the art.' True to his character, he must, however, profess that the speech which he makes is not his own, for he knows nothing of himself. (Compare Symp.) Regarded as a rhetorical exercise, the superiority of his speech seems to consist chiefly in a better arrangement of the topics; he begins with a definition of love, and he gives weight to his words by going back to general maxims; a lesser merit is the greater liveliness of Socrates, which hurries him into verse and relieves the monotony of the style.

But Plato had doubtless a higher purpose than to exhibit Socrates as the rival or superior of the Athenian rhetoricians. Even in the speech of Lysias there is a germ of truth, and this is further developed in the parallel oration of Socrates. First, passionate love is overthrown by the sophistical or interested, and then both yield to that higher view of love which is afterwards revealed to us. The extreme of commonplace is contrasted with the most ideal and imaginative of speculations. Socrates, half in jest and to satisfy his own wild humour, takes the disguise of Lysias, but he is also in profound earnest and in a deeper vein of irony than usual. Having improvised his own speech, which is based upon the model of the preceding, he condemns them both. Yet the condemnation is not to be taken seriously, for he is evidently trying to express an aspect of the truth. To understand him, we must make abstraction of morality and of the Greek manner of regarding the relation of the sexes. In this, as in his other discussions about love, what Plato says of the loves of men must be transferred to the loves of women before we can attach any serious meaning to his words. Had he lived in our times he would have made the transposition himself. But seeing in his own age the impossibility of woman being the intellectual helpmate or friend of man (except in the rare instances of a Diotima or an Aspasia), seeing that, even as to personal beauty, her place was taken by young mankind instead of womankind, he tries to work out the problem of love without regard to the distinctions of nature. And full of the evils which he recognized as flowing from the spurious form of love, he proceeds with a deep meaning, though partly in joke, to show that the 'non-lover's' love is better than the 'lover's.'

We may raise the same question in another form: Is marriage preferable with or without love? 'Among ourselves,' as we may say, a little parodying the words of Pausanias in the Symposium, 'there would be one answer to this question: the practice and feeling of some foreign countries appears to be more doubtful.' Suppose a modern Socrates, in defiance of the received notions of society and the sentimental literature of the day, alone against all the writers and readers of novels, to suggest this enquiry, would not the younger 'part of the world be ready to take off its coat and run at him might and main?' (Republic.) Yet, if like Peisthetaerus in Aristophanes, he could persuade the 'birds' to hear him, retiring a little behind a rampart, not of pots and dishes, but of unreadable books, he might have something to say for himself. Might he not argue, 'that a rational being should not follow the dictates of passion in the most important act of his or her life'? Who would willingly enter into a contract at first sight, almost without thought, against the advice and opinion of his friends, at a time when he acknowledges that he is not in his right mind? And yet they are praised by the authors of romances, who reject the warnings of their friends or parents, rather than those who listen to them in such matters. Two inexperienced persons, ignorant of the world and of one another, how can they be said to choose?—they draw lots, whence also the saying, 'marriage is a lottery.' Then he would describe their way of life after marriage; how they monopolize one another's affections to the exclusion of friends and relations: how they pass their days in unmeaning fondness or trivial conversation; how the inferior of the two drags the other down to his or her level; how the cares of a family 'breed meanness in their souls.' In the fulfilment of military or public duties, they are not helpers but hinderers of one another: they cannot undertake any noble enterprise, such as makes the names of men and women famous, from domestic considerations. Too late their eyes are opened; they were taken unawares and desire to part company. Better, he would say, a 'little love at the beginning,' for heaven might have increased it; but now their foolish fondness has changed into mutual dislike. In the days of their honeymoon they never understood that they must provide against offences, that they must have interests, that they must learn the art of living as well as loving. Our misogamist will not appeal to Anacreon or Sappho for a confirmation of his view, but to the universal experience of mankind. How much nobler, in conclusion, he will say, is friendship, which does not receive unmeaning praises from novelists and poets, is not exacting or exclusive, is not impaired by familiarity, is much less expensive, is not so likely to take offence, seldom changes, and may be dissolved from time to time without the assistance of the courts. Besides, he will remark that there is a much greater choice of friends than of wives—you may have more of them and they will be far more improving to your mind. They will not keep you dawdling at home, or dancing attendance upon them; or withdraw you from the great world and stirring scenes of life and action which would make a man of you.

In such a manner, turning the seamy side outwards, a modern Socrates might describe the evils of married and domestic life. They are evils which mankind in general have agreed to conceal, partly because they are compensated by greater goods. Socrates or Archilochus would soon have to sing a palinode for the injustice done to lovely Helen, or some misfortune worse than blindness might be fall them. Then they would take up their parable again and say:—that there were two loves, a higher and a lower, holy and unholy, a love of the mind and a love of the body.

'Let me not to the marriage of true minds
Admit impediments. Love is not love
Which alters when it alteration finds.

Love's not time's fool, though rosy lips and cheeks
Within his bending sickle's compass come;
Love alters not with his brief hours and weeks,
But bears it out even to the edge of doom.'

But this true love of the mind cannot exist between two souls, until they are purified from the grossness of earthly passion: they must pass through a time of trial and conflict first; in the language of religion they must be converted or born again. Then they would see the world transformed into a scene of heavenly beauty; a divine idea would accompany them in all their thoughts and actions. Something too of the recollections of childhood might float about them still; they might regain that old simplicity which had been theirs in other days at their first entrance on life. And although their love of one another was ever present to them, they would acknowledge also a higher love of duty and of God, which united them. And their happiness would depend upon their preserving in them this principle—not losing the ideals of justice and holiness and truth, but renewing them at the fountain of light. When they have attained to this exalted state, let them marry (something too may be conceded to the animal nature of man): or live together in holy and innocent friendship. The poet might describe in eloquent words the nature of such a union; how after many struggles the true love was found: how the two passed their lives together in the service of God and man; how their characters were reflected upon one another, and seemed to grow more like year by year; how they read in one another's eyes the thoughts, wishes, actions of the other; how they saw each other in God; how in a figure they grew wings like doves, and were 'ready to fly away together and be at rest.' And lastly, he might tell how, after a time at no long intervals, first one and then the other fell asleep, and 'appeared to the unwise' to die, but were reunited in another state of being, in which they saw justice and holiness and truth, not according to the imperfect copies of them which are found in this world, but justice absolute in existence absolute, and so of the rest. And they would hold converse not only with each other, but with blessed souls everywhere; and would be employed in the service of God, every soul fulfilling his own nature and character, and would see into the wonders of earth and heaven, and trace the works of creation to their author.

So, partly in jest but also 'with a certain degree of seriousness,' we may appropriate to ourselves the words of Plato. The use of such a parody, though very imperfect, is to transfer his thoughts to our sphere of religion and feeling, to bring him nearer to us and us to him. Like the Scriptures, Plato admits of endless applications, if we allow for the difference of times and manners; and we lose the better half of him when we regard his Dialogues merely as literary compositions. Any ancient work which is worth reading has a practical and speculative as well as a literary interest. And in Plato, more than in any other Greek writer, the local and transitory is inextricably blended with what is spiritual and eternal. Socrates is necessarily ironical; for he has to withdraw from the received opinions and beliefs of mankind. We cannot separate the transitory from the permanent; nor can we translate the language of irony into that of plain reflection and common sense. But we can imagine the mind of Socrates in another age and country; and we can interpret him by analogy with reference to the errors and prejudices which prevail among ourselves. To return to the Phaedrus:—

Both speeches are strongly condemned by Socrates as sinful and blasphemous towards the god Love, and as worthy only of some haunt of sailors to which good manners were unknown. The meaning of this and other wild language to the same effect, which is introduced by way of contrast to the formality of the two speeches (Socrates has a sense of relief when he has escaped from the trammels of rhetoric), seems to be that the two speeches proceed upon the supposition that love is and ought to be interested, and that no such thing as a real or disinterested passion, which would be at the same time lasting, could be conceived. 'But did I call this "love"? O God, forgive my blasphemy. This is not love. Rather it is the love of the world. But there is another kingdom of love, a kingdom not of this world, divine, eternal. And this other love I will now show you in a mystery.'

Then follows the famous myth, which is a sort of parable, and like other parables ought not to receive too minute an interpretation. In all such allegories there is a great deal which is merely ornamental, and the interpreter has to separate the important from the unimportant. Socrates himself has given the right clue when, in using his own discourse afterwards as the text for his examination of rhetoric, he characterizes it as a 'partly true and tolerably credible mythus,' in which amid poetical figures, order and arrangement were not forgotten.

The soul is described in magnificent language as the self-moved and the source of motion in all other things. This is the philosophical theme or proem of the whole. But ideas must be given through something, and under the pretext that to realize the true nature of the soul would be not only tedious but impossible, we at once pass on to describe the souls of gods as well as men under the figure of two winged steeds and a charioteer. No connection is traced between the soul as the great motive power and the triple soul which is thus imaged. There is no difficulty in seeing that the charioteer represents the reason, or that the black horse is the symbol of the sensual or concupiscent element of human nature. The white horse also represents rational impulse, but the description, 'a lover of honour and modesty and temperance, and a follower of true glory,' though similar, does not at once recall the 'spirit' (thumos) of the Republic. The two steeds really correspond in a figure more nearly to the appetitive and moral or semi-rational soul of Aristotle. And thus, for the first time perhaps in the history of philosophy, we have represented to us the threefold division of psychology. The image of the charioteer and the steeds has been compared with a similar image which occurs in the verses of Parmenides; but it is important to remark that the horses of Parmenides have no allegorical meaning, and that the poet is only describing his own approach in a chariot to the regions of light and the house of the goddess of truth.

The triple soul has had a previous existence, in which following in the train of some god, from whom she derived her character, she beheld partially and imperfectly the vision of absolute truth. All her after existence, passed in many forms of men and animals, is spent in regaining this. The stages of the conflict are many and various; and she is sorely let and hindered by the animal desires of the inferior or concupiscent steed. Again and again she beholds the flashing beauty of the beloved. But before that vision can be finally enjoyed the animal desires must be subjected.

The moral or spiritual element in man is represented by the immortal steed which, like thumos in the Republic, always sides with the reason. Both are dragged out of their course by the furious impulses of desire. In the end something is conceded to the desires, after they have been finally humbled and overpowered. And yet the way of philosophy, or perfect love of the unseen, is total abstinence from bodily delights. 'But all men cannot receive this saying': in the lower life of ambition they may be taken off their guard and stoop to folly unawares, and then, although they do not attain to the highest bliss, yet if they have once conquered they may be happy enough.

The language of the Meno and the Phaedo as well as of the Phaedrus seems to show that at one time of his life Plato was quite serious in maintaining a former state of existence. His mission was to realize the abstract; in that, all good and truth, all the hopes of this and another life seemed to centre. To him abstractions, as we call them, were another kind of knowledge— an inner and unseen world, which seemed to exist far more truly than the fleeting objects of sense which were without him. When we are once able to imagine the intense power which abstract ideas exercised over the mind of Plato, we see that there was no more difficulty to him in realizing the eternal existence of them and of the human minds which were associated with them, in the past and future than in the present. The difficulty was not how they could exist, but how they could fail to exist. In the attempt to regain this 'saving' knowledge of the ideas, the sense was found to be as great an enemy as the desires; and hence two things which to us seem quite distinct are inextricably blended in the representation of Plato.

Thus far we may believe that Plato was serious in his conception of the soul as a motive power, in his reminiscence of a former state of being, in his elevation of the reason over sense and passion, and perhaps in his doctrine of transmigration. Was he equally serious in the rest? For example, are we to attribute his tripartite division of the soul to the gods? Or is this merely assigned to them by way of parallelism with men? The latter is the more probable; for the horses of the gods are both white, i.e. their every impulse is in harmony with reason; their dualism, on the other hand, only carries out the figure of the chariot. Is he serious, again, in regarding love as 'a madness'? That seems to arise out of the antithesis to the former conception of love. At the same time he appears to intimate here, as in the Ion, Apology, Meno, and elsewhere, that there is a faculty in man, whether to be termed in modern language genius, or inspiration, or imagination, or idealism, or communion with God, which cannot be reduced to rule and measure. Perhaps, too, he is ironically repeating the common language of mankind about philosophy, and is turning their jest into a sort of earnest. (Compare Phaedo, Symp.) Or is he serious in holding that each soul bears the character of a god? He may have had no other account to give of the differences of human characters to which he afterwards refers. Or, again, in his absurd derivation of mantike and oionistike and imeros (compare Cratylus)? It is characteristic of the irony of Socrates to mix up sense and nonsense in such a way that no exact line can be drawn between them. And allegory helps to increase this sort of confusion.

As is often the case in the parables and prophecies of Scripture, the meaning is allowed to break through the figure, and the details are not always consistent. When the charioteers and their steeds stand upon the dome of heaven they behold the intangible invisible essences which are not objects of sight. This is because the force of language can no further go. Nor can we dwell much on the circumstance, that at the completion of ten thousand years all are to return to the place from whence they came; because he represents their return as dependent on their own good conduct in the successive stages of existence. Nor again can we attribute anything to the accidental inference which would also follow, that even a tyrant may live righteously in the condition of life to which fate has called him ('he aiblins might, I dinna ken'). But to suppose this would be at variance with Plato himself and with Greek notions generally. He is much more serious in distinguishing men from animals by their recognition of the universal which they have known in a former state, and in denying that this gift of reason can ever be obliterated or lost. In the language of some modern theologians he might be said to maintain the 'final perseverance' of those who have entered on their pilgrim's progress. Other intimations of a 'metaphysic' or 'theology' of the future may also be discerned in him: (1) The moderate predestinarianism which here, as in the Republic, acknowledges the element of chance in human life, and yet asserts the freedom and responsibility of man; (2) The recognition of a moral as well as an intellectual principle in man under the image of an immortal steed; (3) The notion that the divine nature exists by the contemplation of ideas of virtue and justice—or, in other words, the assertion of the essentially moral nature of God; (4) Again, there is the hint that human life is a life of aspiration only, and that the true ideal is not to be found in art; (5) There occurs the first trace of the distinction between necessary and contingent matter; (6) The conception of the soul itself as the motive power and reason of the universe.

The conception of the philosopher, or the philosopher and lover in one, as a sort of madman, may be compared with the Republic and Theaetetus, in both of which the philosopher is regarded as a stranger and monster upon the earth. The whole myth, like the other myths of Plato, describes in a figure things which are beyond the range of human faculties, or inaccessible to the knowledge of the age. That philosophy should be represented as the inspiration of love is a conception that has already become familiar to us in the Symposium, and is the expression partly of Plato's enthusiasm for the idea, and is also an indication of the real power exercised by the passion of friendship over the mind of the Greek. The master in the art of love knew that there was a mystery in these feelings and their associations, and especially in the contrast of the sensible and permanent which is afforded by them; and he sought to explain this, as he explained universal ideas, by a reference to a former state of existence. The capriciousness of love is also derived by him from an attachment to some god in a former world. The singular remark that the beloved is more affected than the lover at the final consummation of their love, seems likewise to hint at a psychological truth.

It is difficult to exhaust the meanings of a work like the Phaedrus, which indicates so much more than it expresses; and is full of inconsistencies and ambiguities which were not perceived by Plato himself. For example, when he is speaking of the soul does he mean the human or the divine soul? and are they both equally self-moving and constructed on the same threefold principle? We should certainly be disposed to reply that the self-motive is to be attributed to God only; and on the other hand that the appetitive and passionate elements have no place in His nature. So we should infer from the reason of the thing, but there is no indication in Plato's own writings that this was his meaning. Or, again, when he explains the different characters of men by referring them back to the nature of the God whom they served in a former state of existence, we are inclined to ask whether he is serious: Is he not rather using a mythological figure, here as elsewhere, to draw a veil over things which are beyond the limits of mortal knowledge? Once more, in speaking of beauty is he really thinking of some external form such as might have been expressed in the works of Phidias or Praxiteles; and not rather of an imaginary beauty, of a sort which extinguishes rather than stimulates vulgar love,—a heavenly beauty like that which flashed from time to time before the eyes of Dante or Bunyan? Surely the latter. But it would be idle to reconcile all the details of the passage: it is a picture, not a system, and a picture which is for the greater part an allegory, and an allegory which allows the meaning to come through. The image of the charioteer and his steeds is placed side by side with the absolute forms of justice, temperance, and the like, which are abstract ideas only, and which are seen with the eye of the soul in her heavenly journey. The first impression of such a passage, in which no attempt is made to separate the substance from the form, is far truer than an elaborate philosophical analysis.

It is too often forgotten that the whole of the second discourse of Socrates is only an allegory, or figure of speech. For this reason, it is unnecessary to enquire whether the love of which Plato speaks is the love of men or of women. It is really a general idea which includes both, and in which the sensual element, though not wholly eradicated, is reduced to order and measure. We must not attribute a meaning to every fanciful detail. Nor is there any need to call up revolting associations, which as a matter of good taste should be banished, and which were far enough away from the mind of Plato. These and similar passages should be interpreted by the Laws. Nor is there anything in the Symposium, or in the Charmides, in reality inconsistent with the sterner rule which Plato lays down in the Laws. At the same time it is not to be denied that love and philosophy are described by Socrates in figures of speech which would not be used in Christian times; or that nameless vices were prevalent at Athens and in other Greek cities; or that friendships between men were a more sacred tie, and had a more important social and educational influence than among ourselves. (See note on Symposium.)

In the Phaedrus, as well as in the Symposium, there are two kinds of love, a lower and a higher, the one answering to the natural wants of the animal, the other rising above them and contemplating with religious awe the forms of justice, temperance, holiness, yet finding them also 'too dazzling bright for mortal eye,' and shrinking from them in amazement. The opposition between these two kinds of love may be compared to the opposition between the flesh and the spirit in the Epistles of St. Paul. It would be unmeaning to suppose that Plato, in describing the spiritual combat, in which the rational soul is finally victor and master of both the steeds, condescends to allow any indulgence of unnatural lusts.

Two other thoughts about love are suggested by this passage. First of all, love is represented here, as in the Symposium, as one of the great powers of nature, which takes many forms and two principal ones, having a predominant influence over the lives of men. And these two, though opposed, are not absolutely separated the one from the other. Plato, with his great knowledge of human nature, was well aware how easily one is transformed into the other, or how soon the noble but fleeting aspiration may return into the nature of the animal, while the lower instinct which is latent always remains. The intermediate sentimentalism, which has exercised so great an influence on the literature of modern Europe, had no place in the classical times of Hellas; the higher love, of which Plato speaks, is the subject, not of poetry or fiction, but of philosophy.

Secondly, there seems to be indicated a natural yearning of the human mind that the great ideas of justice, temperance, wisdom, should be expressed in some form of visible beauty, like the absolute purity and goodness which Christian art has sought to realize in the person of the Madonna. But although human nature has often attempted to represent outwardly what can be only 'spiritually discerned,' men feel that in pictures and images, whether painted or carved, or described in words only, we have not the substance but the shadow of the truth which is in heaven. There is no reason to suppose that in the fairest works of Greek art, Plato ever conceived himself to behold an image, however faint, of ideal truths. 'Not in that way was wisdom seen.'

We may now pass on to the second part of the Dialogue, which is a criticism on the first. Rhetoric is assailed on various grounds: first, as desiring to persuade, without a knowledge of the truth; and secondly, as ignoring the distinction between certain and probable matter. The three speeches are then passed in review: the first of them has no definition of the nature of love, and no order in the topics (being in these respects far inferior to the second); while the third of them is found (though a fancy of the hour) to be framed upon real dialectical principles. But dialectic is not rhetoric; nothing on that subject is to be found in the endless treatises of rhetoric, however prolific in hard names. When Plato has sufficiently put them to the test of ridicule he touches, as with the point of a needle, the real error, which is the confusion of preliminary knowledge with creative power. No attainments will provide the speaker with genius; and the sort of attainments which can alone be of any value are the higher philosophy and the power of psychological analysis, which is given by dialectic, but not by the rules of the rhetoricians.

In this latter portion of the Dialogue there are many texts which may help us to speak and to think. The names dialectic and rhetoric are passing out of use; we hardly examine seriously into their nature and limits, and probably the arts both of speaking and of conversation have been unduly neglected by us. But the mind of Socrates pierces through the differences of times and countries into the essential nature of man; and his words apply equally to the modern world and to the Athenians of old. Would he not have asked of us, or rather is he not asking of us, Whether we have ceased to prefer appearances to reality? Let us take a survey of the professions to which he refers and try them by his standard. Is not all literature passing into criticism, just as Athenian literature in the age of Plato was degenerating into sophistry and rhetoric? We can discourse and write about poems and paintings, but we seem to have lost the gift of creating them. Can we wonder that few of them 'come sweetly from nature,' while ten thousand reviewers (mala murioi) are engaged in dissecting them? Young men, like Phaedrus, are enamoured of their own literary clique and have but a feeble sympathy with the master-minds of former ages. They recognize 'a POETICAL necessity in the writings of their favourite author, even when he boldly wrote off just what came in his head.' They are beginning to think that Art is enough, just at the time when Art is about to disappear from the world. And would not a great painter, such as Michael Angelo, or a great poet, such as Shakespeare, returning to earth, 'courteously rebuke' us—would he not say that we are putting 'in the place of Art the preliminaries of Art,' confusing Art the expression of mind and truth with Art the composition of colours and forms; and perhaps he might more severely chastise some of us for trying to invent 'a new shudder' instead of bringing to the birth living and healthy creations? These he would regard as the signs of an age wanting in original power.

Turning from literature and the arts to law and politics, again we fall under the lash of Socrates. For do we not often make 'the worse appear the better cause;' and do not 'both parties sometimes agree to tell lies'? Is not pleading 'an art of speaking unconnected with the truth'? There is another text of Socrates which must not be forgotten in relation to this subject. In the endless maze of English law is there any 'dividing the whole into parts or reuniting the parts into a whole'—any semblance of an organized being 'having hands and feet and other members'? Instead of a system there is the Chaos of Anaxagoras (omou panta chremata) and no Mind or Order. Then again in the noble art of politics, who thinks of first principles and of true ideas? We avowedly follow not the truth but the will of the many (compare Republic). Is not legislation too a sort of literary effort, and might not statesmanship be described as the 'art of enchanting' the house? While there are some politicians who have no knowledge of the truth, but only of what is likely to be approved by 'the many who sit in judgment,' there are others who can give no form to their ideal, neither having learned 'the art of persuasion,' nor having any insight into the 'characters of men.' Once more, has not medical science become a professional routine, which many 'practise without being able to say who were their instructors'— the application of a few drugs taken from a book instead of a life-long study of the natures and constitutions of human beings? Do we see as clearly as Hippocrates 'that the nature of the body can only be understood as a whole'? (Compare Charm.) And are not they held to be the wisest physicians who have the greatest distrust of their art? What would Socrates think of our newspapers, of our theology? Perhaps he would be afraid to speak of them;—the one vox populi, the other vox Dei, he might hesitate to attack them; or he might trace a fanciful connexion between them, and ask doubtfully, whether they are not equally inspired? He would remark that we are always searching for a belief and deploring our unbelief, seeming to prefer popular opinions unverified and contradictory to unpopular truths which are assured to us by the most certain proofs: that our preachers are in the habit of praising God 'without regard to truth and falsehood, attributing to Him every species of greatness and glory, saying that He is all this and the cause of all that, in order that we may exhibit Him as the fairest and best of all' (Symp.) without any consideration of His real nature and character or of the laws by which He governs the world—seeking for a 'private judgment' and not for the truth or 'God's judgment.' What would he say of the Church, which we praise in like manner, 'meaning ourselves,' without regard to history or experience? Might he not ask, whether we 'care more for the truth of religion, or for the speaker and the country from which the truth comes'? or, whether the 'select wise' are not 'the many' after all? (Symp.) So we may fill up the sketch of Socrates, lest, as Phaedrus says, the argument should be too 'abstract and barren of illustrations.' (Compare Symp., Apol., Euthyphro.)

He next proceeds with enthusiasm to define the royal art of dialectic as the power of dividing a whole into parts, and of uniting the parts in a whole, and which may also be regarded (compare Soph.) as the process of the mind talking with herself. The latter view has probably led Plato to the paradox that speech is superior to writing, in which he may seem also to be doing an injustice to himself. For the two cannot be fairly compared in the manner which Plato suggests. The contrast of the living and dead word, and the example of Socrates, which he has represented in the form of the Dialogue, seem to have misled him. For speech and writing have really different functions; the one is more transitory, more diffuse, more elastic and capable of adaptation to moods and times; the other is more permanent, more concentrated, and is uttered not to this or that person or audience, but to all the world. In the Politicus the paradox is carried further; the mind or will of the king is preferred to the written law; he is supposed to be the Law personified, the ideal made Life.

Yet in both these statements there is also contained a truth; they may be compared with one another, and also with the other famous paradox, that 'knowledge cannot be taught.' Socrates means to say, that what is truly written is written in the soul, just as what is truly taught grows up in the soul from within and is not forced upon it from without. When planted in a congenial soil the little seed becomes a tree, and 'the birds of the air build their nests in the branches.' There is an echo of this in the prayer at the end of the Dialogue, 'Give me beauty in the inward soul, and may the inward and outward man be at one.' We may further compare the words of St. Paul, 'Written not on tables of stone, but on fleshly tables of the heart;' and again, 'Ye are my epistles known and read of all men.' There may be a use in writing as a preservative against the forgetfulness of old age, but to live is higher far, to be ourselves the book, or the epistle, the truth embodied in a person, the Word made flesh. Something like this we may believe to have passed before Plato's mind when he affirmed that speech was superior to writing. So in other ages, weary of literature and criticism, of making many books, of writing articles in reviews, some have desired to live more closely in communion with their fellow-men, to speak heart to heart, to speak and act only, and not to write, following the example of Socrates and of Christ...

Some other touches of inimitable grace and art and of the deepest wisdom may be also noted; such as the prayer or 'collect' which has just been cited, 'Give me beauty,' etc.; or 'the great name which belongs to God alone;' or 'the saying of wiser men than ourselves that a man of sense should try to please not his fellow-servants, but his good and noble masters,' like St. Paul again; or the description of the 'heavenly originals'...

The chief criteria for determining the date of the Dialogue are (1) the ages of Lysias and Isocrates; (2) the character of the work.

Lysias was born in the year 458; Isocrates in the year 436, about seven years before the birth of Plato. The first of the two great rhetoricians is described as in the zenith of his fame; the second is still young and full of promise. Now it is argued that this must have been written in the youth of Isocrates, when the promise was not yet fulfilled. And thus we should have to assign the Dialogue to a year not later than 406, when Isocrates was thirty and Plato twenty-three years of age, and while Socrates himself was still alive.

Those who argue in this way seem not to reflect how easily Plato can 'invent Egyptians or anything else,' and how careless he is of historical truth or probability. Who would suspect that the wise Critias, the virtuous Charmides, had ended their lives among the thirty tyrants? Who would imagine that Lysias, who is here assailed by Socrates, is the son of his old friend Cephalus? Or that Isocrates himself is the enemy of Plato and his school? No arguments can be drawn from the appropriateness or inappropriateness of the characters of Plato. (Else, perhaps, it might be further argued that, judging from their extant remains, insipid rhetoric is far more characteristic of Isocrates than of Lysias.) But Plato makes use of names which have often hardly any connection with the historical characters to whom they belong. In this instance the comparative favour shown to Isocrates may possibly be accounted for by the circumstance of his belonging to the aristocratical, as Lysias to the democratical party.

Few persons will be inclined to suppose, in the superficial manner of some ancient critics, that a dialogue which treats of love must necessarily have been written in youth. As little weight can be attached to the argument that Plato must have visited Egypt before he wrote the story of Theuth and Thamus. For there is no real proof that he ever went to Egypt; and even if he did, he might have known or invented Egyptian traditions before he went there. The late date of the Phaedrus will have to be established by other arguments than these: the maturity of the thought, the perfection of the style, the insight, the relation to the other Platonic Dialogues, seem to contradict the notion that it could have been the work of a youth of twenty or twenty-three years of age. The cosmological notion of the mind as the primum mobile, and the admission of impulse into the immortal nature, also afford grounds for assigning a later date. (Compare Tim., Soph., Laws.) Add to this that the picture of Socrates, though in some lesser particulars,—e.g. his going without sandals, his habit of remaining within the walls, his emphatic declaration that his study is human nature,—an exact resemblance, is in the main the Platonic and not the real Socrates. Can we suppose 'the young man to have told such lies' about his master while he was still alive? Moreover, when two Dialogues are so closely connected as the Phaedrus and Symposium, there is great improbability in supposing that one of them was written at least twenty years after the other. The conclusion seems to be, that the Dialogue was written at some comparatively late but unknown period of Plato's life, after he had deserted the purely Socratic point of view, but before he had entered on the more abstract speculations of the Sophist or the Philebus. Taking into account the divisions of the soul, the doctrine of transmigration, the contemplative nature of the philosophic life, and the character of the style, we shall not be far wrong in placing the Phaedrus in the neighbourhood of the Republic; remarking only that allowance must be made for the poetical element in the Phaedrus, which, while falling short of the Republic in definite philosophic results, seems to have glimpses of a truth beyond.

Two short passages, which are unconnected with the main subject of the Dialogue, may seem to merit a more particular notice: (1) the locus classicus about mythology; (2) the tale of the grasshoppers.

The first passage is remarkable as showing that Plato was entirely free from what may be termed the Euhemerism of his age. For there were Euhemerists in Hellas long before Euhemerus. Early philosophers, like Anaxagoras and Metrodorus, had found in Homer and mythology hidden meanings. Plato, with a truer instinct, rejects these attractive interpretations; he regards the inventor of them as 'unfortunate;' and they draw a man off from the knowledge of himself. There is a latent criticism, and also a poetical sense in Plato, which enable him to discard them, and yet in another way to make use of poetry and mythology as a vehicle of thought and feeling. What would he have said of the discovery of Christian doctrines in these old Greek legends? While acknowledging that such interpretations are 'very nice,' would he not have remarked that they are found in all sacred literatures? They cannot be tested by any criterion of truth, or used to establish any truth; they add nothing to the sum of human knowledge; they are—what we please, and if employed as 'peacemakers' between the new and old are liable to serious misconstruction, as he elsewhere remarks (Republic). And therefore he would have 'bid Farewell to them; the study of them would take up too much of his time; and he has not as yet learned the true nature of religion.' The 'sophistical' interest of Phaedrus, the little touch about the two versions of the story, the ironical manner in which these explanations are set aside—'the common opinion about them is enough for me'—the allusion to the serpent Typho may be noted in passing; also the general agreement between the tone of this speech and the remark of Socrates which follows afterwards, 'I am a diviner, but a poor one.'

The tale of the grasshoppers is naturally suggested by the surrounding scene. They are also the representatives of the Athenians as children of the soil. Under the image of the lively chirruping grasshoppers who inform the Muses in heaven about those who honour them on earth, Plato intends to represent an Athenian audience (tettigessin eoikotes). The story is introduced, apparently, to mark a change of subject, and also, like several other allusions which occur in the course of the Dialogue, in order to preserve the scene in the recollection of the reader.

No one can duly appreciate the dialogues of Plato, especially the Phaedrus, Symposium, and portions of the Republic, who has not a sympathy with mysticism. To the uninitiated, as he would himself have acknowledged, they will appear to be the dreams of a poet who is disguised as a philosopher. There is a twofold difficulty in apprehending this aspect of the Platonic writings. First, we do not immediately realize that under the marble exterior of Greek literature was concealed a soul thrilling with spiritual emotion. Secondly, the forms or figures which the Platonic philosophy assumes, are not like the images of the prophet Isaiah, or of the Apocalypse, familiar to us in the days of our youth. By mysticism we mean, not the extravagance of an erring fancy, but the concentration of reason in feeling, the enthusiastic love of the good, the true, the one, the sense of the infinity of knowledge and of the marvel of the human faculties. When feeding upon such thoughts the 'wing of the soul' is renewed and gains strength; she is raised above 'the manikins of earth' and their opinions, waiting in wonder to know, and working with reverence to find out what God in this or in another life may reveal to her.

ON THE DECLINE OF GREEK LITERATURE.

One of the main purposes of Plato in the Phaedrus is to satirize Rhetoric, or rather the Professors of Rhetoric who swarmed at Athens in the fourth century before Christ. As in the opening of the Dialogue he ridicules the interpreters of mythology; as in the Protagoras he mocks at the Sophists; as in the Euthydemus he makes fun of the word-splitting Eristics; as in the Cratylus he ridicules the fancies of Etymologers; as in the Meno and Gorgias and some other dialogues he makes reflections and casts sly imputation upon the higher classes at Athens; so in the Phaedrus, chiefly in the latter part, he aims his shafts at the rhetoricians. The profession of rhetoric was the greatest and most popular in Athens, necessary 'to a man's salvation,' or at any rate to his attainment of wealth or power; but Plato finds nothing wholesome or genuine in the purpose of it. It is a veritable 'sham,' having no relation to fact, or to truth of any kind. It is antipathetic to him not only as a philosopher, but also as a great writer. He cannot abide the tricks of the rhetoricians, or the pedantries and mannerisms which they introduce into speech and writing. He sees clearly how far removed they are from the ways of simplicity and truth, and how ignorant of the very elements of the art which they are professing to teach. The thing which is most necessary of all, the knowledge of human nature, is hardly if at all considered by them. The true rules of composition, which are very few, are not to be found in their voluminous systems. Their pretentiousness, their omniscience, their large fortunes, their impatience of argument, their indifference to first principles, their stupidity, their progresses through Hellas accompanied by a troop of their disciples—these things were very distasteful to Plato, who esteemed genius far above art, and was quite sensible of the interval which separated them (Phaedrus). It is the interval which separates Sophists and rhetoricians from ancient famous men and women such as Homer and Hesiod, Anacreon and Sappho, Aeschylus and Sophocles; and the Platonic Socrates is afraid that, if he approves the former, he will be disowned by the latter. The spirit of rhetoric was soon to overspread all Hellas; and Plato with prophetic insight may have seen, from afar, the great literary waste or dead level, or interminable marsh, in which Greek literature was soon to disappear. A similar vision of the decline of the Greek drama and of the contrast of the old literature and the new was present to the mind of Aristophanes after the death of the three great tragedians (Frogs). After about a hundred, or at most two hundred years if we exclude Homer, the genius of Hellas had ceased to flower or blossom. The dreary waste which follows, beginning with the Alexandrian writers and even before them in the platitudes of Isocrates and his school, spreads over much more than a thousand years. And from this decline the Greek language and literature, unlike the Latin, which has come to life in new forms and been developed into the great European languages, never recovered.

This monotony of literature, without merit, without genius and without character, is a phenomenon which deserves more attention than it has hitherto received; it is a phenomenon unique in the literary history of the world. How could there have been so much cultivation, so much diligence in writing, and so little mind or real creative power? Why did a thousand years invent nothing better than Sibylline books, Orphic poems, Byzantine imitations of classical histories, Christian reproductions of Greek plays, novels like the silly and obscene romances of Longus and Heliodorus, innumerable forged epistles, a great many epigrams, biographies of the meanest and most meagre description, a sham philosophy which was the bastard progeny of the union between Hellas and the East? Only in Plutarch, in Lucian, in Longinus, in the Roman emperors Marcus Aurelius and Julian, in some of the Christian fathers are there any traces of good sense or originality, or any power of arousing the interest of later ages. And when new books ceased to be written, why did hosts of grammarians and interpreters flock in, who never attain to any sound notion either of grammar or interpretation? Why did the physical sciences never arrive at any true knowledge or make any real progress? Why did poetry droop and languish? Why did history degenerate into fable? Why did words lose their power of expression? Why were ages of external greatness and magnificence attended by all the signs of decay in the human mind which are possible?

To these questions many answers may be given, which if not the true causes, are at least to be reckoned among the symptoms of the decline. There is the want of method in physical science, the want of criticism in history, the want of simplicity or delicacy in poetry, the want of political freedom, which is the true atmosphere of public speaking, in oratory. The ways of life were luxurious and commonplace. Philosophy had become extravagant, eclectic, abstract, devoid of any real content. At length it ceased to exist. It had spread words like plaster over the whole field of knowledge. It had grown ascetic on one side, mystical on the other. Neither of these tendencies was favourable to literature. There was no sense of beauty either in language or in art. The Greek world became vacant, barbaric, oriental. No one had anything new to say, or any conviction of truth. The age had no remembrance of the past, no power of understanding what other ages thought and felt. The Catholic faith had degenerated into dogma and controversy. For more than a thousand years not a single writer of first-rate, or even of second-rate, reputation has a place in the innumerable rolls of Greek literature.

If we seek to go deeper, we can still only describe the outward nature of the clouds or darkness which were spread over the heavens during so many ages without relief or light. We may say that this, like several other long periods in the history of the human race, was destitute, or deprived of the moral qualities which are the root of literary excellence. It had no life or aspiration, no national or political force, no desire for consistency, no love of knowledge for its own sake. It did not attempt to pierce the mists which surrounded it. It did not propose to itself to go forward and scale the heights of knowledge, but to go backwards and seek at the beginning what can only be found towards the end. It was lost in doubt and ignorance. It rested upon tradition and authority. It had none of the higher play of fancy which creates poetry; and where there is no true poetry, neither can there be any good prose. It had no great characters, and therefore it had no great writers. It was incapable of distinguishing between words and things. It was so hopelessly below the ancient standard of classical Greek art and literature that it had no power of understanding or of valuing them. It is doubtful whether any Greek author was justly appreciated in antiquity except by his own contemporaries; and this neglect of the great authors of the past led to the disappearance of the larger part of them, while the Greek fathers were mostly preserved. There is no reason to suppose that, in the century before the taking of Constantinople, much more was in existence than the scholars of the Renaissance carried away with them to Italy.

The character of Greek literature sank lower as time went on. It consisted more and more of compilations, of scholia, of extracts, of commentaries, forgeries, imitations. The commentator or interpreter had no conception of his author as a whole, and very little of the context of any passage which he was explaining. The least things were preferred by him to the greatest. The question of a reading, or a grammatical form, or an accent, or the uses of a word, took the place of the aim or subject of the book. He had no sense of the beauties of an author, and very little light is thrown by him on real difficulties. He interprets past ages by his own. The greatest classical writers are the least appreciated by him. This seems to be the reason why so many of them have perished, why the lyric poets have almost wholly disappeared; why, out of the eighty or ninety tragedies of Aeschylus and Sophocles, only seven of each had been preserved.

Such an age of sciolism and scholasticism may possibly once more get the better of the literary world. There are those who prophesy that the signs of such a day are again appearing among us, and that at the end of the present century no writer of the first class will be still alive. They think that the Muse of Literature may transfer herself to other countries less dried up or worn out than our own. They seem to see the withering effect of criticism on original genius. No one can doubt that such a decay or decline of literature and of art seriously affects the manners and character of a nation. It takes away half the joys and refinements of life; it increases its dulness and grossness. Hence it becomes a matter of great interest to consider how, if at all, such a degeneracy may be averted. Is there any elixir which can restore life and youth to the literature of a nation, or at any rate which can prevent it becoming unmanned and enfeebled?

First there is the progress of education. It is possible, and even probable, that the extension of the means of knowledge over a wider area and to persons living under new conditions may lead to many new combinations of thought and language. But, as yet, experience does not favour the realization of such a hope or promise. It may be truly answered that at present the training of teachers and the methods of education are very imperfect, and therefore that we cannot judge of the future by the present. When more of our youth are trained in the best literatures, and in the best parts of them, their minds may be expected to have a larger growth. They will have more interests, more thoughts, more material for conversation; they will have a higher standard and begin to think for themselves. The number of persons who will have the opportunity of receiving the highest education through the cheap press, and by the help of high schools and colleges, may increase tenfold. It is likely that in every thousand persons there is at least one who is far above the average in natural capacity, but the seed which is in him dies for want of cultivation. It has never had any stimulus to grow, or any field in which to blossom and produce fruit. Here is a great reservoir or treasure-house of human intelligence out of which new waters may flow and cover the earth. If at any time the great men of the world should die out, and originality or genius appear to suffer a partial eclipse, there is a boundless hope in the multitude of intelligences for future generations. They may bring gifts to men such as the world has never received before. They may begin at a higher point and yet take with them all the results of the past. The co-operation of many may have effects not less striking, though different in character from those which the creative genius of a single man, such as Bacon or Newton, formerly produced. There is also great hope to be derived, not merely from the extension of education over a wider area, but from the continuance of it during many generations. Educated parents will have children fit to receive education; and these again will grow up under circumstances far more favourable to the growth of intelligence than any which have hitherto existed in our own or in former ages.

Even if we were to suppose no more men of genius to be produced, the great writers of ancient or of modern times will remain to furnish abundant materials of education to the coming generation. Now that every nation holds communication with every other, we may truly say in a fuller sense than formerly that 'the thoughts of men are widened with the process of the suns.' They will not be 'cribbed, cabined, and confined' within a province or an island. The East will provide elements of culture to the West as well as the West to the East. The religions and literatures of the world will be open books, which he who wills may read. The human race may not be always ground down by bodily toil, but may have greater leisure for the improvement of the mind. The increasing sense of the greatness and infinity of nature will tend to awaken in men larger and more liberal thoughts. The love of mankind may be the source of a greater development of literature than nationality has ever been. There may be a greater freedom from prejudice and party; we may better understand the whereabouts of truth, and therefore there may be more success and fewer failures in the search for it. Lastly, in the coming ages we shall carry with us the recollection of the past, in which are necessarily contained many seeds of revival and renaissance in the future. So far is the world from becoming exhausted, so groundless is the fear that literature will ever die out.

PHAEDRUS

PERSONS OF THE DIALOGUE: Socrates, Phaedrus.
SCENE: Under a plane-tree, by the banks of the Ilissus.

SOCRATES: My dear Phaedrus, whence come you, and whither are you going?

PHAEDRUS: I come from Lysias the son of Cephalus, and I am going to take a walk outside the wall, for I have been sitting with him the whole morning; and our common friend Acumenus tells me that it is much more refreshing to walk in the open air than to be shut up in a cloister.

SOCRATES: There he is right. Lysias then, I suppose, was in the town?

PHAEDRUS: Yes, he was staying with Epicrates, here at the house of Morychus; that house which is near the temple of Olympian Zeus.

SOCRATES: And how did he entertain you? Can I be wrong in supposing that Lysias gave you a feast of discourse?

PHAEDRUS: You shall hear, if you can spare time to accompany me.

SOCRATES: And should I not deem the conversation of you

and Lysias 'a thing of higher import,' as I may say in the words of Pindar, 'than any business'?

PHAEDRUS: Will you go on?

SOCRATES: And will you go on with the narration?

PHAEDRUS: My tale, Socrates, is one of your sort, for love was the theme which occupied us—love after a fashion: Lysias has been writing about a fair youth who was being tempted, but not by a lover; and this was the point: he ingeniously proved that the non-lover should be accepted rather than the lover.

SOCRATES: O that is noble of him! I wish that he would say the poor man rather than the rich, and the old man rather than the young one;—then he would meet the case of me and of many a man; his words would be quite refreshing, and he would be a public benefactor. For my part, I do so long to hear his speech, that if you walk all the way to Megara, and when you have reached the wall come back, as Herodicus recommends, without going in, I will keep you company.

PHAEDRUS: What do you mean, my good Socrates? How can you imagine that my unpractised memory can do justice to an elaborate work, which the greatest rhetorician of the age spent a long time in composing. Indeed, I cannot; I would give a great deal if I could.

SOCRATES: I believe that I know Phaedrus about as well as I know myself, and I am very sure that the speech of Lysias was repeated to him, not once only, but again and again;—he insisted on hearing it many times over and Lysias was very willing to gratify him; at last, when nothing else would do, he got hold of the book, and looked at what he most wanted to see,—this occupied him during the whole morning;—and then when he was tired with sitting, he went out to take a walk, not until, by the dog, as I believe, he had simply learned by heart the entire discourse, unless it was unusually long, and he went to a place outside the wall that he might practise his lesson. There he saw a certain lover of discourse who had a similar weakness;—he saw and rejoiced; now thought he, 'I shall have a partner in my revels.' And he invited him to come and walk with him. But when the lover of discourse begged that he would repeat the tale, he gave himself airs and said, 'No I cannot,' as if he were indisposed; although, if the hearer had refused, he would sooner or later have been compelled by him to listen whether he would or no. Therefore, Phaedrus, bid him do at once what he will soon do whether bidden or not.

PHAEDRUS: I see that you will not let me off until I speak in some fashion or other; verily therefore my best plan is to speak as I best can.

SOCRATES: A very true remark, that of yours.

PHAEDRUS: I will do as I say; but believe me, Socrates, I did not learn the very words—O no; nevertheless I have a general notion of what he said, and will give you a summary of the points in which the lover differed from the non-lover. Let me begin at the beginning.

SOCRATES: Yes, my sweet one; but you must first of all show what you have in your left hand under your cloak, for that roll, as I suspect, is the actual discourse. Now, much as I love you, I would not have you suppose that I am going to have your memory exercised at my expense, if you have Lysias himself here.

PHAEDRUS: Enough; I see that I have no hope of practising my art upon you. But if I am to read, where would you please to sit?

SOCRATES: Let us turn aside and go by the Ilissus; we will sit down at some quiet spot.

PHAEDRUS: I am fortunate in not having my sandals, and as you never have any, I think that we may go along the brook and cool our feet in the water; this will be the easiest way, and at midday and in the summer is far from being unpleasant.

SOCRATES: Lead on, and look out for a place in which we can sit down.

PHAEDRUS: Do you see the tallest plane-tree in the distance?
SOCRATES: Yes.

PHAEDRUS: There are shade and gentle breezes, and grass on which we may either sit or lie down.

SOCRATES: Move forward.

PHAEDRUS: I should like to know, Socrates, whether the place is not somewhere here at which Boreas is said to have carried off Orithyia from the banks of the Ilissus?

SOCRATES: Such is the tradition.

PHAEDRUS: And is this the exact spot? The little stream is delightfully clear and bright; I can fancy that there might be maidens playing near.

SOCRATES: I believe that the spot is not exactly here, but about a quarter of a mile lower down, where you cross to the temple of Artemis, and there is, I think, some sort of an altar of Boreas at the place.

PHAEDRUS: I have never noticed it; but I beseech you to tell me, Socrates, do you believe this tale?

SOCRATES: The wise are doubtful, and I should not be singular if, like them, I too doubted. I might have a rational explanation that Orithyia was playing with Pharmacia, when a northern gust carried her over the neighbouring rocks; and this being the manner of her death, she was said to have been carried away by Boreas. There is a discrepancy, however, about the locality; according to another version of the story she was taken from Areopagus, and not from this place. Now I quite acknowledge that these allegories are very nice, but he is not to be envied who has to invent them; much labour and ingenuity will be required of him; and when he has once begun, he must go on and rehabilitate Hippocentaurs and chimeras dire. Gorgons and winged steeds flow in apace, and numberless other inconceivable and portentous natures. And if he is sceptical about them, and would fain reduce them one after another to the rules of probability, this sort of crude philosophy will take up a great deal of time. Now I have no leisure for such enquiries; shall I tell you why? I must first know myself, as the Delphian inscription says; to be curious about that which is not my concern, while I am still in ignorance of my own self, would be ridiculous. And therefore I bid farewell to all this; the common opinion is enough for me. For, as I was saying, I want to know not about this, but about myself: am I a monster more complicated and swollen with passion than the serpent Typho, or a creature of a gentler and simpler sort, to whom Nature has given a diviner and lowlier destiny? But let me ask you, friend: have we not reached the plane-tree to which you were conducting us?

PHAEDRUS: Yes, this is the tree.

SOCRATES: By Here, a fair resting-place, full of summer sounds and scents. Here is this lofty and spreading plane-tree, and the agnus castus high and clustering, in the fullest blossom and the greatest fragrance; and the stream which flows beneath the plane-tree is deliciously cold to the feet. Judging from the ornaments and images, this must be a spot sacred to Achelous and the Nymphs. How delightful is the breeze:—so very sweet; and there is a sound in the air shrill and summerlike which makes answer to the chorus of the cicadae. But the greatest charm of all is the grass, like a pillow gently sloping to the head. My dear Phaedrus, you have been an admirable guide.

PHAEDRUS: What an incomprehensible being you are, Socrates: when you are in the country, as you say, you really are like some stranger who is led about by a guide. Do you ever cross the border? I rather think that you never venture even outside the gates.

SOCRATES: Very true, my good friend; and I hope that you will excuse me when you hear the reason, which is, that I am a lover of knowledge, and the men who dwell in the city are my teachers, and not the trees or the country. Though I do indeed believe that you have found a spell with which to draw me out of the city into the country, like a hungry cow before whom a bough or a bunch of fruit is waved. For only hold up before me in like manner a book, and you may lead me all round Attica, and over the wide world. And now having arrived, I intend to lie down, and do you choose any posture in which you can read best. Begin.

PHAEDRUS: Listen. You know how matters stand with me; and how, as I conceive, this affair may be arranged for the advantage of both of us. And I maintain that I ought not to fail in my suit, because I am not your lover: for lovers repent of the kindnesses which they have shown when their passion ceases, but to the non-lovers who are free and not under any compulsion, no time of repentance ever comes; for they confer their benefits according to the measure of their ability, in the way which is most conducive to their own interest. Then again, lovers consider how by reason of their love they have neglected their own concerns and rendered service to others: and when to these benefits conferred they add on the troubles which they have endured, they think that they have long ago made to the beloved a very ample return. But the non-lover has no such tormenting recollections; he has never neglected his affairs or quarrelled with his relations; he has no troubles to add up or excuses to invent; and being well rid of all these evils, why should he not freely do what will gratify the beloved? If you say that the lover is more to be esteemed, because his love is thought to be greater; for he is willing to say and do what is hateful to other men, in order to please his beloved;—that, if true, is only a proof that he will prefer any future love to his present, and will injure his old love at the pleasure of the new. And how, in a matter of such infinite importance, can a man be right in trusting himself to one who is afflicted with a malady which no experienced person would attempt to cure, for the patient himself admits that he is not in his right mind, and acknowledges that he is wrong in his mind, but says that he is unable to control himself? And if he came to his right mind, would he ever imagine that the desires were good which he conceived when in his wrong mind? Once more, there are many more non-lovers than lovers; and if you choose the best of the lovers, you will not have many to choose from; but if from the non-lovers, the choice will be larger, and you will be far more likely to find among them a person who is worthy of your friendship. If public opinion be your dread, and you would avoid reproach, in all probability the lover, who is always thinking that other men are as emulous of him as he is of them, will boast to some one of his successes, and make a show of them openly in the pride of his heart;—he wants others to know that his labour has not been lost; but the non-lover is more his own master, and is desirous of solid good, and not of the opinion of mankind. Again, the lover may be generally noted or seen following the beloved (this is his regular occupation), and whenever they are observed to exchange two words they are supposed to meet about some affair of love either past or in contemplation; but when non-lovers meet, no one asks the reason why, because people know that talking to another is natural, whether friendship or mere pleasure be the motive. Once more, if you fear the fickleness of friendship, consider that in any other case a quarrel might be a mutual calamity; but now, when you have given up what is most precious to you, you will be the greater loser, and therefore, you will have more reason in being afraid of the lover, for his vexations are many, and he is always fancying that every one is leagued against him. Wherefore also he debars his beloved from society; he will not have you intimate with the wealthy, lest they should exceed him in wealth, or with men of education, lest they should be his superiors in understanding; and he is equally afraid of anybody's influence who has any other advantage over himself. If he can persuade you to break with them, you are left without a friend in the world; or if, out of a regard to your own interest, you have more sense than to comply with his desire, you will have to quarrel with him. But those who are non-lovers, and whose success in love is the reward of their merit, will not be jealous of the companions of their beloved, and will rather hate those who refuse to be his associates, thinking that their favourite is slighted by the latter and benefited by the former; for more love than hatred may be expected to come to him out of his friendship with others. Many lovers too have loved the person of a youth before they knew his character or his belongings; so that when their passion has passed away, there is no knowing whether they will continue to be his friends; whereas, in the case of non-lovers who were always friends, the friendship is not lessened by the favours granted; but the recollection of these remains with them, and is an earnest of good things to come.

Further, I say that you are likely to be improved by me, whereas the lover will spoil you. For they praise your words and actions in a wrong way; partly, because they are afraid of offending you, and also, their judgment is weakened by passion. Such are the feats which love exhibits; he makes things painful to the disappointed which give no pain to others; he compels the successful lover to praise what ought not to give him pleasure, and therefore the beloved is to be pitied rather than envied. But if you listen to me, in the first place, I, in my intercourse with you, shall not merely regard present enjoyment, but also future advantage, being not mastered by love, but my own master; nor for small causes taking violent dislikes, but even when the cause is great, slowly laying up little wrath—unintentional offences I shall forgive, and intentional ones I shall try to prevent; and these are the marks of a friendship which will last.

Do you think that a lover only can be a firm friend? reflect:—if this were true, we should set small value on sons, or fathers, or mothers; nor should we ever have loyal friends, for our love of them arises not from passion, but from other associations. Further, if we ought to shower favours on those who are the most eager suitors,—on that principle, we ought always to do good, not to the most virtuous, but to the most needy; for they are the persons who will be most relieved, and will therefore be the most grateful; and when you make a feast you should invite not your friend, but the beggar and the empty soul; for they will love you, and attend you, and come about your doors, and will be the best pleased, and the most grateful, and will invoke many a blessing on your head. Yet surely you ought not to be granting favours to those who besiege you with prayer, but to those who are best able to reward you; nor to the lover only, but to those who are worthy of love; nor to those who will enjoy the bloom of your youth, but to those who will share their possessions with you in age; nor to those who, having succeeded, will glory in their success to others, but to those who will be modest and tell no tales; nor to those who care about you for a moment only, but to those who will continue your friends through life; nor to those who, when their passion is over, will pick a quarrel with you, but rather to those who, when the charm of youth has left you, will show their own virtue. Remember what I have said; and consider yet this further point: friends admonish the lover under the idea that his way of life is bad, but no one of his kindred ever yet censured the non-lover, or thought that he was ill-advised about his own interests.

'Perhaps you will ask me whether I propose that you should indulge every non-lover. To which I reply that not even the lover would advise you to indulge all lovers, for the indiscriminate favour is less esteemed by the rational recipient, and less easily hidden by him who would escape the censure of the world. Now love ought to be for the advantage of both parties, and for the injury of neither.

'I believe that I have said enough; but if there is anything more which you desire or which in your opinion needs to be supplied, ask and I will answer.'

Now, Socrates, what do you think? Is not the discourse excellent, more especially in the matter of the language?

SOCRATES: Yes, quite admirable; the effect on me was ravishing. And this I owe to you, Phaedrus, for I observed you while reading to be in an ecstasy, and thinking that you are more experienced in these matters than I am, I followed your example, and, like you, my divine darling, I became inspired with a phrenzy.

PHAEDRUS: Indeed, you are pleased to be merry.

SOCRATES: Do you mean that I am not in earnest?

PHAEDRUS: Now don't talk in that way, Socrates, but let me have your real opinion; I adjure you, by Zeus, the god of friendship, to tell me whether you think that any Hellene could have said more or spoken better on the same subject.

SOCRATES: Well, but are you and I expected to praise the sentiments of the author, or only the clearness, and roundness, and finish, and tournure of the language? As to the first I willingly submit to your better judgment, for I am not worthy to form an opinion, having only attended to the rhetorical manner; and I was doubting whether this could have been defended even by Lysias himself; I thought, though I speak under correction, that he repeated himself two or three times, either from want of words or from want of pains; and also, he appeared to me ostentatiously to exult in showing how well he could say the same thing in two or three ways.

PHAEDRUS: Nonsense, Socrates; what you call repetition was the especial merit of the speech; for he omitted no topic of which the subject rightly allowed, and I do not think that any one could have spoken better or more exhaustively.

SOCRATES: There I cannot go along with you. Ancient sages, men and women, who have spoken and written of these things, would rise up in judgment against me, if out of complaisance I assented to you.

PHAEDRUS: Who are they, and where did you hear anything better than this?

SOCRATES: I am sure that I must have heard; but at this moment I do not remember from whom; perhaps from Sappho the fair, or Anacreon the wise; or, possibly, from a prose writer. Why do I say so? Why, because I perceive that my bosom is full, and that I could make another speech as good as that of Lysias, and different. Now I am certain that this is not an invention of my own, who am well aware that I know nothing, and therefore I can only infer that I have been filled through the ears, like a pitcher, from the waters of another, though I have actually forgotten in my stupidity who was my informant.

PHAEDRUS: That is grand:—but never mind where you heard the discourse or from whom; let that be a mystery not to be divulged even at my earnest desire. Only, as you say, promise to make another and better oration, equal in length and entirely new, on the same subject; and I, like the nine Archons, will promise to set up a golden image at Delphi, not only of myself, but of you, and as large as life.

SOCRATES: You are a dear golden ass if you suppose me to mean that Lysias has altogether missed the mark, and that I can make a speech from which all his arguments are to be excluded. The worst of authors will say something which is to the point. Who, for example, could speak on this thesis of yours without praising the discretion of the non-lover and blaming the indiscretion of the lover? These are the commonplaces of the subject which must come in (for what else is there to be said?) and must be allowed and excused; the only merit is in the arrangement of them, for there can be none in the invention; but when you leave the commonplaces, then there may be some originality.

PHAEDRUS: I admit that there is reason in what you say, and I too will be reasonable, and will allow you to start with the premiss that the lover is more disordered in his wits than the non-lover; if in what remains you make a longer and better speech than Lysias, and use other arguments, then I say again, that a statue you shall have of beaten gold, and take your place by the colossal offerings of the Cypselids at Olympia.

SOCRATES: How profoundly in earnest is the lover, because to tease him I lay a finger upon his love! And so, Phaedrus, you really imagine that I am going to improve upon the ingenuity of Lysias?

PHAEDRUS: There I have you as you had me, and you must just speak 'as you best can.' Do not let us exchange 'tu quoque' as in a farce, or compel me to say to you as you said to me, 'I know Socrates as well as I know myself, and he was wanting to speak, but he gave himself airs.' Rather I would have you consider that from this place we stir not until you have unbosomed yourself of the speech; for here are we all alone, and I am stronger, remember, and younger than you:—Wherefore perpend, and do not compel me to use violence.

SOCRATES: But, my sweet Phaedrus, how ridiculous it would be of me to compete with Lysias in an extempore speech! He is a master in his art and I am an untaught man.

PHAEDRUS: You see how matters stand; and therefore let there be no more pretences; for, indeed, I know the word that is irresistible.

SOCRATES: Then don't say it.

PHAEDRUS: Yes, but I will; and my word shall be an oath. 'I say, or rather swear'—but what god will be witness of my oath? —'By this plane-tree I swear, that unless you repeat the discourse here in the face of this very plane-tree, I will never tell you another; never let you have word of another!'

SOCRATES: Villain! I am conquered; the poor lover of discourse has no more to say.

PHAEDRUS: Then why are you still at your tricks?

SOCRATES: I am not going to play tricks now that you have taken the oath, for I cannot allow myself to be starved.

PHAEDRUS: Proceed.

SOCRATES: Shall I tell you what I will do?

PHAEDRUS: What?

SOCRATES: I will veil my face and gallop through the discourse as fast as I can, for if I see you I shall feel ashamed and not know what to say.

PHAEDRUS: Only go on and you may do anything else which you please.

SOCRATES: Come, O ye Muses, melodious, as ye are called, whether you have received this name from the character of your strains, or because the Melians are a musical race, help, O help me in the tale which my good friend here desires me to rehearse, in order that his friend whom he always deemed wise may seem to him to be wiser than ever.

Once upon a time there was a fair boy, or, more properly speaking, a youth; he was very fair and had a great many lovers; and there was one special cunning one, who had persuaded the youth that he did not love him, but he really loved him all the same; and one day when he was paying his addresses to him, he used this very argument—that he ought to accept the non-lover rather than the lover; his words were as follows:—

'All good counsel begins in the same way; a man should know what he is advising about, or his counsel will all come to nought. But people imagine that they know about the nature of things, when they don't know about them, and, not having come to an understanding at first because they think that they know, they end, as might be expected, in contradicting one another and themselves. Now you and I must not be guilty of this fundamental error which we condemn in others; but as our question is whether the lover or non-lover is to be preferred, let us first of all agree in defining the nature and power of love, and then, keeping our eyes upon the definition and to this appealing, let us further enquire whether love brings advantage or disadvantage.

'Every one sees that love is a desire, and we know also that non-lovers desire the beautiful and good. Now in what way is the lover to be distinguished from the non-lover? Let us note that in every one of us there are two guiding and ruling principles which lead us whither they will; one is the natural desire of pleasure, the other is an acquired opinion which aspires after the best; and these two are sometimes in harmony and then again at war, and sometimes the one, sometimes the other conquers. When opinion by the help of reason leads us to the best, the conquering principle is called temperance; but when desire, which is devoid of reason, rules in us and drags us to pleasure, that power of misrule is called excess. Now excess has many names, and many members, and many forms, and any of these forms when very marked gives a name, neither honourable nor creditable, to the bearer of the name. The desire of eating, for example, which gets the better of the higher reason and the other desires, is called gluttony, and he who is possessed by it is called a glutton; the tyrannical desire of drink, which inclines the possessor of the desire to drink, has a name which is only too obvious, and there can be as little doubt by what name any other appetite of the same family would be called;—it will be the name of that which happens to be dominant. And now I think that you will perceive the drift of my discourse; but as every spoken word is in a manner plainer than the unspoken, I had better say further that the irrational desire which overcomes the tendency of opinion towards right, and is led away to the enjoyment of beauty, and especially of personal beauty, by the desires which are her own kindred—that supreme desire, I say, which by leading conquers and by the force of passion is reinforced, from this very force, receiving a name, is called love (erromenos eros).'

And now, dear Phaedrus, I shall pause for an instant to ask whether you do not think me, as I appear to myself, inspired?

PHAEDRUS: Yes, Socrates, you seem to have a very unusual flow of words.

SOCRATES: Listen to me, then, in silence; for surely the place is holy; so that you must not wonder, if, as I proceed, I appear to be in a divine fury, for already I am getting into dithyrambics.

PHAEDRUS: Nothing can be truer.

SOCRATES: The responsibility rests with you. But hear what follows, and perhaps the fit may be averted; all is in their hands above. I will go on talking to my youth. Listen:—

Thus, my friend, we have declared and defined the nature of the subject. Keeping the definition in view, let us now enquire what advantage or disadvantage is likely to ensue from the lover or the non-lover to him who accepts their advances.

He who is the victim of his passions and the slave of pleasure will of course desire to make his beloved as agreeable to himself as possible. Now to him who has a mind diseased anything is agreeable which is not opposed to him, but that which is equal or superior is hateful to him, and therefore the lover will not brook any superiority or equality on the part of his beloved; he is always employed in reducing him to inferiority. And the ignorant is the inferior of the wise, the coward of the brave, the slow of speech of the speaker, the dull of the clever. These, and not these only, are the mental defects of the beloved;—defects which, when implanted by nature, are necessarily a delight to the lover, and when not implanted, he must contrive to implant them in him, if he would not be deprived of his fleeting joy. And therefore he cannot help being jealous, and will debar his beloved from the advantages of society which would make a man of him, and especially from that society which would have given him wisdom, and thereby he cannot fail to do him great harm. That is to say, in his excessive fear lest he should come to be despised in his eyes he will be compelled to banish from him divine philosophy; and there is no greater injury which he can inflict upon him than this. He will contrive that his beloved shall be wholly ignorant, and in everything shall look to him; he is to be the delight of the lover's heart, and a curse to himself. Verily, a lover is a profitable guardian and associate for him in all that relates to his mind.

Let us next see how his master, whose law of life is pleasure and not good, will keep and train the body of his servant. Will he not choose a beloved who is delicate rather than sturdy and strong? One brought up in shady bowers and not in the bright sun, a stranger to manly exercises and the sweat of toil, accustomed only to a soft and luxurious diet, instead of the hues of health having the colours of paint and ornament, and the rest of a piece?—such a life as any one can imagine and which I need not detail at length. But I may sum up all that I have to say in a word, and pass on. Such a person in war, or in any of the great crises of life, will be the anxiety of his friends and also of his lover, and certainly not the terror of his enemies; which nobody can deny.

And now let us tell what advantage or disadvantage the beloved will receive from the guardianship and society of his lover in the matter of his property; this is the next point to be considered. The lover will be the first to see what, indeed, will be sufficiently evident to all men, that he desires above all things to deprive his beloved of his dearest and best and holiest possessions, father, mother, kindred, friends, of all whom he thinks may be hinderers or reprovers of their most sweet converse; he will even cast a jealous eye upon his gold and silver or other property, because these make him a less easy prey, and when caught less manageable; hence he is of necessity displeased at his possession of them and rejoices at their loss; and he would like him to be wifeless, childless, homeless, as well; and the longer the better, for the longer he is all this, the longer he will enjoy him.

There are some sort of animals, such as flatterers, who are dangerous and mischievous enough, and yet nature has mingled a temporary pleasure and grace in their composition. You may say that a courtesan is hurtful, and disapprove of such creatures and their practices, and yet for the time they are very pleasant. But the lover is not only hurtful to his love; he is also an extremely disagreeable companion. The old proverb says that 'birds of a feather flock together'; I suppose that equality of years inclines them to the same pleasures, and similarity begets friendship; yet you may have more than enough even of this; and verily constraint is always said to be grievous. Now the lover is not only unlike his beloved, but he forces himself upon him. For he is old and his love is young, and neither day nor night will he leave him if he can help; necessity and the sting of desire drive him on, and allure him with the pleasure which he receives from seeing, hearing, touching, perceiving him in every way. And therefore he is delighted to fasten upon him and to minister to him. But what pleasure or consolation can the beloved be receiving all this time? Must he not feel the extremity of disgust when he looks at an old shrivelled face and the remainder to match, which even in a description is disagreeable, and quite detestable when he is forced into daily contact with his lover; moreover he is jealously watched and guarded against everything and everybody, and has to hear misplaced and exaggerated praises of himself, and censures equally inappropriate, which are intolerable when the man is sober, and, besides being intolerable, are published all over the world in all their indelicacy and wearisomeness when he is drunk.

And not only while his love continues is he mischievous and unpleasant, but when his love ceases he becomes a perfidious enemy of him on whom he showered his oaths and prayers and promises, and yet could hardly prevail upon him to tolerate the tedium of his company even from motives of interest. The hour of payment arrives, and now he is the servant of another master; instead of love and infatuation, wisdom and temperance are his bosom's lords; but the beloved has not discovered the change which has taken place in him, when he asks for a return and recalls to his recollection former sayings and doings; he believes himself to be speaking to the same person, and the other, not having the courage to confess the truth, and not knowing how to fulfil the oaths and promises which he made when under the dominion of folly, and having now grown wise and temperate, does not want to do as he did or to be as he was before. And so he runs away and is constrained to be a defaulter; the oyster-shell (In allusion to a game in which two parties fled or pursued according as an oyster-shell which was thrown into the air fell with the dark or light side uppermost.) has fallen with the other side uppermost —he changes pursuit into flight, while the other is compelled to follow him with passion and imprecation, not knowing that he ought never from the first to have accepted a demented lover instead of a sensible non-lover; and that in making such a choice he was giving himself up to a faithless, morose, envious, disagreeable being, hurtful to his estate, hurtful to his bodily health, and still more hurtful to the cultivation of his mind, than which there neither is nor ever will be anything more honoured in the eyes both of gods and men. Consider this, fair youth, and know that in the friendship of the lover there is no real kindness; he has an appetite and wants to feed upon you:

'As wolves love lambs so lovers love their loves.'

But I told you so, I am speaking in verse, and therefore I had better make an end; enough.

PHAEDRUS: I thought that you were only half-way and were going to make a similar speech about all the advantages of accepting the non-lover. Why do you not proceed?

SOCRATES: Does not your simplicity observe that I have got

out of dithyrambics into heroics, when only uttering a censure on the lover? And if I am to add the praises of the non-lover what will become of me? Do you not perceive that I am already overtaken by the Nymphs to whom you have mischievously exposed me? And therefore I will only add that the non-lover has all the advantages in which the lover is accused of being deficient. And now I will say no more; there has been enough of both of them. Leaving the tale to its fate, I will cross the river and make the best of my way home, lest a worse thing be inflicted upon me by you.

PHAEDRUS: Not yet, Socrates; not until the heat of the day has passed; do you not see that the hour is almost noon? there is the midday sun standing still, as people say, in the meridian. Let us rather stay and talk over what has been said, and then return in the cool.

SOCRATES: Your love of discourse, Phaedrus, is superhuman, simply marvellous, and I do not believe that there is any one of your contemporaries who has either made or in one way or another has compelled others to make an equal number of speeches. I would except Simmias the Theban, but all the rest are far behind you. And now I do verily believe that you have been the cause of another.

PHAEDRUS: That is good news. But what do you mean?

SOCRATES: I mean to say that as I was about to cross the stream the usual sign was given to me,—that sign which always forbids, but never bids, me to do anything which I am going to do; and I thought that I heard a voice saying in my ear that I had been guilty of impiety, and that I must not go away until I had made an atonement. Now I am a diviner, though not a very good one, but I have enough religion for my own use, as you might say of a bad writer—his writing is good enough for him; and I am beginning to see that I was in error. O my friend, how prophetic is the human soul! At the time I had a sort of misgiving, and, like Ibycus, 'I was troubled; I feared that I might be buying honour from men at the price of sinning against the gods.' Now I recognize my error.

PHAEDRUS: What error?

SOCRATES: That was a dreadful speech which you brought with you, and you made me utter one as bad.

PHAEDRUS: How so?

SOCRATES: It was foolish, I say,—to a certain extent, impious; can anything be more dreadful?

PHAEDRUS: Nothing, if the speech was really such as you describe.

SOCRATES: Well, and is not Eros the son of Aphrodite, and a god?

PHAEDRUS: So men say.

SOCRATES: But that was not acknowledged by Lysias in his speech, nor by you in that other speech which you by a charm drew from my lips. For if love be, as he surely is, a divinity, he cannot be evil. Yet this was the error of both the speeches. There was also a simplicity about them which was refreshing; having no truth or honesty in them, nevertheless they pretended to be something, hoping to succeed in deceiving the manikins of earth and gain celebrity among them. Wherefore I must have a purgation. And I bethink me of an ancient purgation of mythological error which was devised, not by Homer, for he never had the wit to discover why he was blind, but by Stesichorus, who was a philosopher and knew the reason why; and therefore, when he lost his eyes, for that was the penalty which was inflicted upon him for reviling the lovely Helen, he at once purged himself. And the purgation was a recantation, which began thus,—

> *'False is that word of mine—the truth is that thou didst*
> *not embark in*
> *ships, nor ever go to the walls of Troy;'*

and when he had completed his poem, which is called 'the

recantation,' immediately his sight returned to him. Now I will be wiser than either Stesichorus or Homer, in that I am going to make my recantation for reviling love before I suffer; and this I will attempt, not as before, veiled and ashamed, but with forehead bold and bare.

PHAEDRUS: Nothing could be more agreeable to me than to hear you say so.

SOCRATES: Only think, my good Phaedrus, what an utter want of delicacy was shown in the two discourses; I mean, in my own and in that which you recited out of the book. Would not any one who was himself of a noble and gentle nature, and who loved or ever had loved a nature like his own, when we tell of the petty causes of lovers' jealousies, and of their exceeding animosities, and of the injuries which they do to their beloved, have imagined that our ideas of love were taken from some haunt of sailors to which good manners were unknown—he would certainly never have admitted the justice of our censure?

PHAEDRUS: I dare say not, Socrates.

SOCRATES: Therefore, because I blush at the thought of this person, and also because I am afraid of Love himself, I desire to wash the brine out of my ears with water from the spring; and I would counsel Lysias not to delay, but to write another discourse, which shall prove that 'ceteris paribus' the lover ought to be accepted rather than the non-lover.

PHAEDRUS: Be assured that he shall. You shall speak the praises of the lover, and Lysias shall be compelled by me to write another discourse on the same theme.

SOCRATES: You will be true to your nature in that, and therefore I believe you.

PHAEDRUS: Speak, and fear not.

SOCRATES: But where is the fair youth whom I was addressing before, and who ought to listen now; lest, if he hear me not, he should accept a non-lover before he knows what he is doing?

PHAEDRUS: He is close at hand, and always at your service.

SOCRATES: Know then, fair youth, that the former discourse was the word of Phaedrus, the son of Vain Man, who dwells in the city of Myrrhina (Myrrhinusius). And this which I am about to utter is the recantation of Stesichorus the son of Godly Man (Euphemus), who comes from the town of Desire (Himera), and is to the following effect: 'I told a lie when I said' that the beloved ought to accept the non-lover when he might have the lover, because the one is sane, and the other mad. It might be so if madness were simply an evil; but there is also a madness which is a divine gift, and the source of the chiefest blessings granted to men. For prophecy is a madness, and the prophetess at Delphi and the priestesses at Dodona when out of their senses have conferred great benefits on Hellas, both in public and private life, but when in their senses few or none. And I might also tell you how the Sibyl and other inspired persons have given to many an one many an intimation of the future which has saved them from falling. But it would be tedious to speak of what every one knows.

There will be more reason in appealing to the ancient inventors of names (compare Cratylus), who would never have connected prophecy (mantike) which foretells the future and is the noblest of arts, with madness (manike), or called them both by the same name, if they had deemed madness to be a disgrace or dishonour;—they must have thought that there was an inspired madness which was a noble thing; for the two words, mantike and manike, are really the same, and the letter tau is only a modern and tasteless insertion. And this is confirmed by the name which was given by them to the rational investigation of futurity, whether made by the help of birds or of other signs—this, for as much as it is an art which supplies from the reasoning faculty mind (nous) and information (istoria) to human thought (oiesis) they originally termed oionoistike, but the word has been lately altered and made sonorous by the modern introduction of the letter Omega (oionoistike and oionistike), and in proportion as prophecy (mantike) is more perfect and august than augury, both in name and fact, in the same proportion, as the ancients testify, is madness superior to a sane mind (sophrosune) for the one is only of human, but the other of divine origin. Again, where plagues and mightiest woes have bred in certain families, owing to some ancient blood-guiltiness, there madness has entered with holy prayers and rites, and by inspired utterances found a way of deliverance for those who are in need; and he who has part in this gift, and is truly possessed and duly out of his mind, is by the use of purifications and mysteries made whole and exempt from evil, future as well as present, and has a release from the calamity which was afflicting him. The third kind is the madness of those who are possessed by the Muses; which taking hold of a delicate and virgin soul, and there inspiring frenzy, awakens lyrical and all other numbers; with these adorning the myriad actions of ancient heroes for the instruction of posterity. But he who, having no touch of the Muses' madness in his soul, comes to the door and thinks that he will get into the temple by the help of art—he, I say, and his poetry are not admitted; the sane man disappears and is nowhere when he enters into rivalry with the madman.

I might tell of many other noble deeds which have sprung from inspired madness. And therefore, let no one frighten or flutter us by saying that the temperate friend is to be chosen rather than the inspired, but let him further show that love is not sent by the gods for any good to lover or beloved; if he can do so we will allow him to carry off the palm. And we, on our part, will prove in answer to him that the madness of love is the greatest of heaven's blessings, and the proof shall be one which the wise will receive, and the witling disbelieve. But first of all, let us view the affections and actions of the soul divine and human, and try to ascertain the truth about them. The beginning of our proof is as follows:—

(Translated by Cic. Tus. Quaest.) The soul through all her being is immortal, for that which is ever in motion is immortal; but that which moves another and is moved by another, in ceasing to move ceases also to live. Only the self-moving, never leaving self, never ceases to move, and is the fountain and beginning of motion to all that moves besides. Now, the beginning is unbegotten, for that which is begotten has a beginning; but the beginning is begotten of nothing, for if it were begotten of something, then the begotten would not come from a beginning. But if unbegotten, it must also be indestructible; for if beginning were destroyed, there could be no beginning out of anything, nor anything out of a beginning; and all things must have a beginning. And therefore the self-moving is the beginning of motion; and this can neither be destroyed nor begotten, else the whole heavens and all creation would collapse and stand still, and never again have motion or birth. But if the self-moving is proved to be immortal, he who affirms that self-motion is the very idea and essence of the soul will not be put to confusion. For the body which is moved from without is soulless; but that which is moved from within has a soul, for such is the nature of the soul. But if this be true, must not the soul be the self-moving, and therefore of necessity unbegotten and immortal? Enough of the soul's immortality.

Of the nature of the soul, though her true form be ever a theme of large and more than mortal discourse, let me speak briefly, and in a figure. And let the figure be composite—a pair of winged horses and a charioteer. Now the winged horses and the charioteers of the gods are all of them noble and of noble descent, but those of other races are mixed; the human charioteer drives his in a pair; and one of them is noble and of noble breed, and the other is ignoble and of ignoble breed; and the driving of them of necessity gives a great deal of trouble to him. I will endeavour to explain to you in what way the mortal differs from the immortal creature. The soul in her totality has the care of inanimate being everywhere, and traverses the whole heaven in divers forms appearing—when perfect and fully winged she soars upward, and orders the whole world; whereas the imperfect soul, losing her wings and drooping in her flight at last settles on the solid ground—there, finding a home, she receives an earthly frame which appears to be self-moved, but is really moved by her power; and this composition of soul and body is called a living and mortal creature. For immortal no such union can be reasonably believed to be; although fancy, not having seen nor surely known the nature of God, may imagine an immortal creature having both a body and also a soul which are united throughout all time. Let that, however, be as God wills, and be spoken of acceptably to him. And now let us ask the reason why the soul loses her wings!

The wing is the corporeal element which is most akin to the divine, and which by nature tends to soar aloft and carry that which gravitates downwards into the upper region, which is the habitation of the gods. The divine is beauty, wisdom, goodness, and the like; and by these the wing of the soul is nourished, and grows apace; but when fed upon evil and foulness and the opposite of good, wastes and falls away. Zeus, the mighty lord, holding the reins of a winged chariot, leads the way in heaven, ordering all and taking care of all; and there follows him the array of gods and demi-gods, marshalled in eleven bands; Hestia alone abides at home in the house of heaven; of the rest they who are reckoned among the princely twelve march in their appointed order. They see many blessed sights in the inner heaven, and there are many ways to and fro, along which the blessed gods are passing, every one doing his own work; he may follow who will and can, for jealousy has no place in the celestial choir. But when they go to banquet and festival, then they move up the steep to the top of the vault of heaven. The chariots of the gods in even poise, obeying the rein, glide rapidly; but the others labour, for the vicious steed goes heavily, weighing down the charioteer to the earth when his steed has not been thoroughly trained:—and this is the hour of agony and extremest conflict for the soul. For the immortals, when they are at the end of their course, go forth and stand upon the outside of heaven, and the revolution of the spheres carries them round, and they behold the things beyond. But of the heaven which is above the heavens, what earthly poet ever did or ever will sing worthily? It is such as I will describe; for

I must dare to speak the truth, when truth is my theme. There abides the very being with which true knowledge is concerned; the colourless, formless, intangible essence, visible only to mind, the pilot of the soul. The divine intelligence, being nurtured upon mind and pure knowledge, and the intelligence of every soul which is capable of receiving the food proper to it, rejoices at beholding reality, and once more gazing upon truth, is replenished and made glad, until the revolution of the worlds brings her round again to the same place. In the revolution she beholds justice, and temperance, and knowledge absolute, not in the form of generation or of relation, which men call existence, but knowledge absolute in existence absolute; and beholding the other true existences in like manner, and feasting upon them, she passes down into the interior of the heavens and returns home; and there the charioteer putting up his horses at the stall, gives them ambrosia to eat and nectar to drink.

Such is the life of the gods; but of other souls, that which follows God best and is likest to him lifts the head of the charioteer into the outer world, and is carried round in the revolution, troubled indeed by the steeds, and with difficulty beholding true being; while another only rises and falls, and sees, and again fails to see by reason of the unruliness of the steeds. The rest of the souls are also longing after the upper world and they all follow, but not being strong enough they are carried round below the surface, plunging, treading on one another, each striving to be first; and there is confusion and perspiration and the extremity of effort; and many of them are lamed or have their wings broken through the ill-driving of the charioteers; and all of them after a fruitless toil, not having attained to the mysteries of true being, go away, and feed upon opinion. The reason why the souls exhibit this exceeding eagerness to behold the plain of truth is that pasturage is found there, which is suited to the highest part of the soul; and the wing on which the soul soars is nourished with this. And there is a law of Destiny, that the soul which attains any vision of truth in company with a god is preserved from harm until the next period, and if attaining always is always unharmed. But when she is unable to follow, and fails to behold the truth, and through some ill-hap sinks beneath the double load of forgetfulness and vice, and her wings fall from her and she drops to the ground, then the law ordains that this soul shall at her first birth pass, not into any other animal, but only into man; and the soul which has seen most of truth shall come to the birth as a philosopher, or artist, or some musical and loving nature; that which has seen truth in the second degree shall be some righteous king or warrior chief; the soul which is of the third class shall be a politician, or economist, or trader; the fourth shall be a lover of gymnastic toils, or a physician; the fifth shall lead the life of a prophet or hierophant; to the sixth the character of poet or some other imitative artist will be assigned; to the seventh the life of an artisan or husbandman; to the eighth that of a sophist or demagogue; to the ninth that of a tyrant—all these are states of probation, in which he who does righteously improves, and he who does unrighteously, deteriorates his lot.

Ten thousand years must elapse before the soul of each one can return to the place from whence she came, for she cannot grow her wings in less; only the soul of a philosopher, guileless and true, or the soul of a lover, who is not devoid of philosophy, may acquire wings in the third of the recurring periods of a thousand years; he is distinguished from the ordinary good man who gains wings in three thousand years:—and they who choose this life three times in succession have wings given them, and go away at the end of three thousand years. But the others (The philosopher alone is not subject to judgment (krisis), for he has never lost the vision of truth.) receive judgment when they have completed their first life, and after the judgment they go, some of them to the houses of correction which are under the earth, and are punished; others to some place in heaven whither they are lightly borne by justice, and there they live in a manner worthy of the life which they led here when in the form of men. And at the end of the first thousand years the good souls and also the evil souls both come to draw lots and choose their second life, and they may take any which they please. The soul of a man may pass into the life of a beast, or from the beast return again into the man. But the soul which has never seen the truth will not pass into the human form. For a man must have intelligence of universals, and be able to proceed from the many particulars of sense to one conception of reason;—this is the recollection of those things which our soul once saw while following God—when regardless of that which we now call being she raised her head up towards the true being. And therefore the mind of the philosopher alone has wings; and this is just, for he is always, according to the measure of his abilities, clinging in recollection to those things in which God abides, and in beholding which He is what He is. And he who employs aright these memories is ever being initiated into perfect mysteries and alone becomes truly perfect. But, as he forgets earthly interests and is rapt in the divine, the vulgar deem him mad, and rebuke him; they do not see that he is inspired.

Thus far I have been speaking of the fourth and last kind of madness, which is imputed to him who, when he sees the beauty of earth, is transported with the recollection of the true beauty; he would like to fly away, but he cannot; he is like a bird fluttering and looking upward and careless of the world below; and he is therefore thought to be mad. And I have shown this of all inspirations to be the noblest and highest and the offspring of the highest to him who has or shares in it, and that he who loves the beautiful is called a lover because he partakes of it. For, as has been already said, every soul of man has in the way of nature beheld true being; this was the condition of her passing into the form of man. But all souls do not easily recall the things of the other world; they may have seen them for a short time only, or they may have been unfortunate in their earthly lot, and, having had their hearts turned to unrighteousness through some corrupting influence, they may have lost the memory of the holy things which once they saw. Few only retain an adequate remembrance of them; and they, when they behold here any image of that other world, are rapt in amazement; but they are ignorant of what this rapture means, because they do not clearly perceive. For there is no light of justice or temperance or any of the higher ideas which are precious to souls in the earthly copies of them: they are seen through a glass dimly; and there are few who, going to the images, behold in them the realities, and these only with difficulty. There was a time when with the rest of the happy band they saw beauty shining in brightness,—we philosophers following in the train of Zeus, others in company with other gods; and then we beheld the beatific vision and were initiated into a mystery which may be truly called most blessed, celebrated by us in our state of innocence, before we had any experience of evils to come, when we were admitted to the sight of apparitions innocent and simple and calm and happy, which we beheld shining in pure light, pure ourselves and not yet enshrined in that living tomb which we carry about, now that we are imprisoned in the body, like an oyster in his shell. Let me linger over the memory of scenes which have passed away.

But of beauty, I repeat again that we saw her there shining in company with the celestial forms; and coming to earth we find her here too, shining in clearness through the clearest aperture of sense. For sight is the most piercing of our bodily senses; though not by that is wisdom seen; her loveliness would have been transporting if there had been a visible image of her, and the other ideas, if they had visible counterparts, would be equally lovely. But this is the privilege of beauty, that being the loveliest she is also the most palpable to sight. Now he who is not newly initiated or who has become corrupted, does not easily rise out of this world to the sight of true beauty in the other; he looks only at her earthly namesake, and instead of being awed at the sight of her, he is given over to pleasure, and like a brutish beast he rushes on to enjoy and beget; he consorts with wantonness, and is not afraid or ashamed of pursuing pleasure in violation of nature. But he whose initiation is recent, and who has been the spectator of many glories in the other world, is amazed when he sees any one having a godlike face or form, which is the expression of divine beauty; and at first a shudder runs through him, and again the old awe steals over him; then looking upon the face of his beloved as of a god he reverences him, and if he were not afraid of being thought a downright madman, he would sacrifice to his beloved as to the image of a god; then while he gazes on him there is a sort of reaction, and the shudder passes into an unusual heat and perspiration; for, as he receives the effluence of beauty through the eyes, the wing moistens and he warms. And as he warms, the parts out of which the wing grew, and which had been hitherto closed and rigid, and had prevented the wing from shooting forth, are melted, and as nourishment streams upon him, the lower end of the wing begins to swell and grow from the root upwards; and the growth extends under the whole soul—for once the whole was winged. During this process the whole soul is all in a state of ebullition and effervescence,—which may be compared to the irritation and uneasiness in the gums at the time of cutting teeth, —bubbles up, and has a feeling of uneasiness and tickling; but when in like manner the soul is beginning to grow wings, the beauty of the beloved meets her eye and she receives the sensible warm motion of particles which flow towards her, therefore called emotion (imeros), and is refreshed and warmed by them, and then she ceases from her pain with joy. But when she is parted from her beloved and her moisture fails, then the orifices of the passage out of which the wing shoots dry up and close, and intercept the germ of the wing; which, being shut up with the emotion, throbbing as with the pulsations of an artery, pricks the aperture which is nearest, until at length the entire soul is pierced and maddened and pained, and at the recollection of beauty is again delighted. And from both of them together the soul is oppressed at the strangeness of her condition, and is in a great strait and excitement, and in her madness can neither sleep by night nor abide in her place by day. And wherever she thinks that she will behold the beautiful one, thither in her desire she runs. And when she has seen him, and bathed herself in the waters of beauty, her constraint is loosened, and she is refreshed, and has no more pangs and pains; and this is the sweetest of all pleasures at the time, and is the reason why the soul of the lover will never forsake his beautiful one, whom he esteems above all; he has forgotten mother and brethren and companions, and he thinks nothing of the neglect and loss of his property; the rules and proprieties of life, on which he formerly prided himself, he now despises, and is ready to sleep like a servant, wherever he is allowed, as near as he can to his desired one, who is the object of his worship, and the physician who can alone assuage the greatness of his pain. And this state, my dear imaginary youth to whom I am talking, is by men called love, and among the gods has a name at which you, in your simplicity, may be inclined to mock; there are two lines in the apocryphal writings of Homer in which the name occurs. One of them is rather outrageous, and not altogether metrical. They are as follows:

'Mortals call him fluttering love, But the immortals call him winged one, Because the growing of wings (Or, reading pterothoiton, 'the movement of wings.') is a necessity to him.'

You may believe this, but not unless you like. At any rate the loves of lovers and their causes are such as I have described.

Now the lover who is taken to be the attendant of Zeus is better able to bear the winged god, and can endure a heavier burden; but the attendants and companions of Ares, when under the influence of love, if they fancy that they have been at all wronged, are ready to kill and put an end to themselves and their beloved. And he who follows in the train of any other god, while he is unspoiled and the impression lasts, honours and imitates him, as far as he is able; and after the manner of his God he behaves in his intercourse with his beloved and with the rest of the world during the first period of his earthly existence. Every one chooses his love from the ranks of beauty according to his character, and this he makes his god, and fashions and adorns as a sort of image which he is to fall down and worship. The followers of Zeus desire that their beloved should have a soul like him; and therefore they seek out some one of a philosophical and imperial nature, and when they have found him and loved him, they do all they can to confirm such a nature in him, and if they have no experience of such a disposition hitherto, they learn of any one who can teach them, and themselves follow in the same way. And they have the less difficulty in finding the nature of their own god in themselves, because they have been compelled to gaze intensely on him; their recollection clings to him, and they become possessed of him, and receive from him their character and disposition, so far as man can participate in God. The qualities of their god they attribute to the beloved, wherefore they love him all the more, and if, like the Bacchic Nymphs, they draw inspiration from Zeus, they pour out their own fountain upon him, wanting to make him as like as possible to their own god. But those who are the followers of Here seek a royal love, and when they have found him they do just the same with him; and in like manner the followers of Apollo, and of every other god walking in the ways of their god, seek a love who is to be made like him whom they serve, and when they have found him, they themselves imitate their god, and persuade their love to do the same, and educate him into the manner and nature of the god as far as they each can; for no feelings of envy or jealousy are entertained by them towards their beloved, but they do their utmost to create in him the greatest likeness of themselves and of the god whom they honour. Thus fair and blissful to the beloved is the desire of the inspired lover, and the initiation of which I speak into the mysteries of true love, if he be captured by the lover and their purpose is effected. Now the beloved is taken captive in the following manner:—

As I said at the beginning of this tale, I divided each soul into three—two horses and a charioteer; and one of the horses was good and the other bad: the division may remain, but I have not yet explained in what the goodness or badness of either consists, and to that I will now proceed. The right-hand horse is upright and cleanly made; he has a lofty neck and an aquiline nose; his colour is white, and his eyes dark; he is a lover of honour and modesty and temperance, and the follower of true glory; he needs no touch of the whip, but is guided by word and admonition only. The other is a crooked lumbering animal, put together anyhow; he has a short thick neck; he is flat-faced and of a dark colour, with grey eyes and blood-red complexion (Or with grey and blood-shot eyes.); the mate of insolence and pride, shag-eared and deaf, hardly yielding to whip and spur. Now when the charioteer beholds the vision of love, and has his whole soul warmed through sense, and is full of the prickings and ticklings of desire, the obedient steed, then as always under the government of shame, refrains from leaping on the beloved; but the other, heedless of the pricks and of the blows of the whip, plunges and runs away, giving all manner of trouble to his companion and the charioteer, whom he forces to approach the beloved and to remember the joys of love. They at first indignantly oppose him and will not be urged on to do terrible and unlawful deeds; but at last, when he persists in plaguing them, they yield and agree to do as he bids them. And now they are at the spot and behold the flashing beauty of the beloved; which when the charioteer sees, his memory is carried to the true beauty, whom he beholds in company with Modesty like an image placed upon a holy pedestal. He sees her, but he is afraid and falls backwards in adoration, and by his fall is compelled to pull back the reins with such violence as to bring both the steeds on their haunches, the one willing and unresisting, the unruly one very unwilling; and when they have gone back a little, the one is overcome with shame and wonder, and his whole soul is bathed in perspiration; the other, when the pain is over which the bridle and the fall had given him, having with difficulty taken breath, is full of wrath and reproaches, which he heaps upon the charioteer and his fellow-steed, for want of courage and manhood, declaring that they have been false to their agreement and guilty of desertion. Again they refuse, and again he urges them on, and will scarce yield to their prayer that he would wait until another time. When the appointed hour comes, they make as if they had forgotten, and he reminds them, fighting and neighing and dragging them on, until at length he on the same thoughts intent, forces them to draw near again. And when they are near he stoops his head and puts up his tail, and takes the bit in his teeth and pulls shamelessly. Then the charioteer is worse off than ever; he falls back like a racer at the barrier, and with a still more violent wrench drags the bit out of the teeth of the wild steed and covers his abusive tongue and jaws with blood, and forces his legs and haunches to the ground and punishes him sorely. And when this has happened several times and the villain has ceased from his wanton way, he is tamed and humbled, and follows the will of the charioteer, and when he sees the beautiful one he is ready to die of fear. And from that time forward the soul of the lover follows the beloved in modesty and holy fear.

And so the beloved who, like a god, has received every true and loyal service from his lover, not in pretence but in reality, being also himself of a nature friendly to his admirer, if in former days he has blushed to own his passion and turned away his lover, because his youthful companions or others slanderously told him that he would be disgraced, now as years advance, at the appointed age and time, is led to receive him into communion. For fate which has ordained that there shall be no friendship among the evil has also ordained that there shall ever be friendship among the good. And the beloved when he has received him into communion and intimacy, is quite amazed at the good-will of the lover; he recognises that the inspired friend is worth all other friends or kinsmen; they have nothing of friendship in them worthy to be compared with his. And when this feeling continues and he is nearer to him and embraces him, in gymnastic exercises and at other times of meeting, then the fountain of that stream, which Zeus when he was in love with Ganymede named Desire, overflows upon the lover, and some enters into his soul, and some when he is filled flows out again; and as a breeze or an echo rebounds from the smooth rocks and returns whence it came, so does the stream of beauty, passing through the eyes which are the windows of the soul, come back to the beautiful one; there arriving and quickening the passages of the wings, watering them and inclining them to grow, and filling the soul of the beloved also with love. And thus he loves, but he knows not what; he does not understand and cannot explain his own state; he appears to have caught the infection of blindness from another; the lover is his mirror in whom he is beholding himself, but he is not aware of this. When he is with the lover, both cease from their pain, but when he is away then he longs as he is longed for, and has love's image, love for love (Anteros) lodging in his breast, which he calls and believes to be not love but friendship only, and his desire is as the desire of the other, but weaker; he wants to see him, touch him, kiss him, embrace him, and probably not long afterwards his desire is accomplished. When they meet, the wanton steed of the lover has a word to say to the charioteer; he would like to have a little pleasure in return for many pains, but the wanton steed of the beloved says not a word, for he is bursting with passion which he understands not;— he throws his arms round the lover and embraces him as his dearest friend; and, when they are side by side, he is not in a state in which he can refuse the lover anything, if he ask him; although his fellow-steed and the charioteer oppose him with the arguments of shame and reason. After this their happiness depends upon their self-control; if the better elements of the mind which lead to order and philosophy prevail, then they pass their life here in happiness and harmony—masters of themselves and orderly—enslaving the vicious and emancipating the virtuous elements of the soul; and when the end comes, they are light and winged for flight, having conquered in one of the three heavenly or truly Olympian victories; nor can human discipline or divine inspiration confer any greater blessing on man than this. If, on the other hand, they leave philosophy and lead the lower life of ambition, then probably, after wine or in some other careless hour, the two wanton animals take the two souls when off their guard and bring them together, and they accomplish that desire of their hearts which to the many is bliss; and this having once enjoyed they continue to enjoy, yet rarely because they have not the approval of the whole soul. They too are dear, but not so dear to one another as the others, either at the time of their love or afterwards. They consider that they have given and taken from each other the most sacred pledges, and they may not break them and fall into enmity. At last they pass out of the body, unwinged, but eager to soar, and thus obtain no mean reward of love and madness. For those who have once begun the heavenward pilgrimage may not go down again to darkness and the journey beneath the earth, but they live in light always; happy companions in their pilgrimage, and when the time comes at which they receive their wings they have the same plumage because of their love.

Thus great are the heavenly blessings which the friendship of a lover will confer upon you, my youth. Whereas the attachment of the non-lover, which is alloyed with a worldly prudence and has worldly and niggardly ways of doling out benefits, will breed in your soul those vulgar qualities which the populace applaud, will send you bowling round the earth during a period of nine thousand years, and leave you a fool in the world below.

And thus, dear Eros, I have made and paid my recantation, as well and as fairly as I could; more especially in the matter of the poetical figures which I was compelled to use, because Phaedrus would have them. And now forgive the past and accept the present, and be gracious and merciful to me, and do not in thine anger deprive me of sight, or take from me the art of love which thou hast given me, but grant that I may be yet more esteemed in the eyes of the fair. And if Phaedrus or I myself said anything rude in our first speeches, blame Lysias, who is the father of the brat, and let us have no more of his progeny; bid him study philosophy, like his brother Polemarchus; and then his lover Phaedrus will no longer halt between two opinions, but will dedicate himself wholly to love and to philosophical discourses.

PHAEDRUS: I join in the prayer, Socrates, and say with you, if this be for my good, may your words come to pass. But why did you make your second oration so much finer than the first? I wonder why. And I begin to be afraid that I shall lose conceit of Lysias, and that he will appear tame in comparison, even if he be willing to put another as fine and as long as yours into the field, which I doubt. For quite lately one of your politicians was abusing him on this very account; and called him a 'speech writer' again and again. So that a feeling of pride may probably induce him to give up writing speeches.

SOCRATES: What a very amusing notion! But I think, my young man, that you are much mistaken in your friend if you imagine that he is frightened at a little noise; and, possibly, you think that his assailant was in earnest?

PHAEDRUS: I thought, Socrates, that he was. And you are aware that the greatest and most influential statesmen are ashamed of writing speeches and leaving them in a written form, lest they should be called Sophists by posterity.

SOCRATES: You seem to be unconscious, Phaedrus, that the 'sweet elbow' (A proverb, like 'the grapes are sour,' applied to pleasures which cannot be had, meaning sweet things which, like the elbow, are out of the reach of the mouth. The promised pleasure turns out to be a long and tedious affair.) of the proverb is really the long arm of the Nile. And you appear to be equally unaware of the fact that this sweet elbow of theirs is also a long arm. For there is nothing of which our great politicians are so fond as of writing speeches and bequeathing them to posterity. And they add their admirers' names at the top of the writing, out of gratitude to them.

PHAEDRUS: What do you mean? I do not understand.

SOCRATES: Why, do you not know that when a politician writes, he begins with the names of his approvers?

PHAEDRUS: How so?

SOCRATES: Why, he begins in this manner: 'Be it enacted by the senate, the people, or both, on the motion of a certain person,' who is our author; and so putting on a serious face, he proceeds to display his own wisdom to his admirers in what is often a long and tedious composition. Now what is that sort of thing but a regular piece of authorship?

PHAEDRUS: True.

SOCRATES: And if the law is finally approved, then the author leaves the theatre in high delight; but if the law is rejected and he is done out of his speech-making, and not thought good enough to write, then he and his party are in mourning.

PHAEDRUS: Very true.

SOCRATES: So far are they from despising, or rather so highly do they value the practice of writing.

PHAEDRUS: No doubt.

SOCRATES: And when the king or orator has the power, as Lycurgus or Solon or Darius had, of attaining an immortality or authorship in a state, is he not thought by posterity, when they see his compositions, and does he not think himself, while he is yet alive, to be a god?

PHAEDRUS: Very true.

SOCRATES: Then do you think that any one of this class, however ill-disposed, would reproach Lysias with being an author?

PHAEDRUS: Not upon your view; for according to you he would be casting a slur upon his own favourite pursuit.

SOCRATES: Any one may see that there is no disgrace in the mere fact of writing.

PHAEDRUS: Certainly not.

SOCRATES: The disgrace begins when a man writes not well, but badly.

PHAEDRUS: Clearly.

SOCRATES: And what is well and what is badly—need we ask Lysias, or any other poet or orator, who ever wrote or will write either a political or any other work, in metre or out of metre, poet or prose writer, to teach us this?

PHAEDRUS: Need we? For what should a man live if not for

the pleasures of discourse? Surely not for the sake of bodily pleasures, which almost always have previous pain as a condition of them, and therefore are rightly called slavish.

SOCRATES: There is time enough. And I believe that the grasshoppers chirruping after their manner in the heat of the sun over our heads are talking to one another and looking down at us. What would they say if they saw that we, like the many, are not conversing, but slumbering at mid-day, lulled by their voices, too indolent to think? Would they not have a right to laugh at us? They might imagine that we were slaves, who, coming to rest at a place of resort of theirs, like sheep lie asleep at noon around the well. But if they see us discoursing, and like Odysseus sailing past them, deaf to their siren voices, they may perhaps, out of respect, give us of the gifts which they receive from the gods that they may impart them to men.

PHAEDRUS: What gifts do you mean? I never heard of any.

SOCRATES: A lover of music like yourself ought surely to have heard the story of the grasshoppers, who are said to have been human beings in an age before the Muses. And when the Muses came and song appeared they were ravished with delight; and singing always, never thought of eating and drinking, until at last in their forgetfulness they died. And now they live again in the grasshoppers; and this is the return which the Muses make to them—they neither hunger, nor thirst, but from the hour of their birth are always singing, and never eating or drinking; and when they die they go and inform the Muses in heaven who honours them on earth. They win the love of Terpsichore for the dancers by their report of them; of Erato for the lovers, and of the other Muses for those who do them honour, according to the several ways of honouring them;—of Calliope the eldest Muse and of Urania who is next to her, for the philosophers, of whose music the grasshoppers make report to them; for these are the Muses who are chiefly concerned with heaven and thought, divine as well as human, and they have the sweetest utterance. For many reasons, then, we ought always to talk and not to sleep at mid-day.

PHAEDRUS: Let us talk.

SOCRATES: Shall we discuss the rules of writing and speech as we were proposing?

PHAEDRUS: Very good.

SOCRATES: In good speaking should not the mind of the speaker know the truth of the matter about which he is going to speak?

PHAEDRUS: And yet, Socrates, I have heard that he who would be an orator has nothing to do with true justice, but only with that which is likely to be approved by the many who sit in judgment; nor with the truly good or honourable, but only with opinion about them, and that from opinion comes persuasion, and not from the truth.

SOCRATES: The words of the wise are not to be set aside; for there is probably something in them; and therefore the meaning of this saying is not hastily to be dismissed.

PHAEDRUS: Very true.

SOCRATES: Let us put the matter thus:—Suppose that I persuaded you to buy a horse and go to the wars. Neither of us knew what a horse was like, but I knew that you believed a horse to be of tame animals the one which has the longest ears.

PHAEDRUS: That would be ridiculous.

SOCRATES: There is something more ridiculous coming:—Suppose, further, that in sober earnest I, having persuaded you of this, went and composed a speech in honour of an ass, whom I entitled a horse beginning: 'A noble animal and a most useful possession, especially in war, and you may get on his back and fight, and he will carry baggage or anything.'

PHAEDRUS: How ridiculous!

SOCRATES: Ridiculous! Yes; but is not even a ridiculous friend better than a cunning enemy?

PHAEDRUS: Certainly.

SOCRATES: And when the orator instead of putting an ass in the place of a horse, puts good for evil, being himself as ignorant of their true nature as the city on which he imposes is ignorant; and having studied the notions of the multitude, falsely persuades them not about 'the shadow of an ass,' which he confounds with a horse, but about good which he confounds with evil,—what will be the harvest which rhetoric will be likely to gather after the sowing of that seed?

PHAEDRUS: The reverse of good.

SOCRATES: But perhaps rhetoric has been getting too roughly handled by us, and she might answer: What amazing nonsense you are talking! As if I forced any man to learn to speak in ignorance of the truth! Whatever my advice may be worth, I should have told him to arrive at the truth first, and then come to me. At the same time I boldly assert that mere knowledge of the truth will not give you the art of persuasion.

PHAEDRUS: There is reason in the lady's defence of herself.

SOCRATES: Quite true; if only the other arguments which remain to be brought up bear her witness that she is an art at all. But I seem to hear them arraying themselves on the opposite side, declaring that she speaks falsely, and that rhetoric is a mere routine and trick, not an art. Lo! a Spartan appears, and says that there never is nor ever will be a real art of speaking which is divorced from the truth.

PHAEDRUS: And what are these arguments, Socrates? Bring them out that we may examine them.

SOCRATES: Come out, fair children, and convince Phaedrus, who is the father of similar beauties, that he will never be able to speak about anything as he ought to speak unless he have a knowledge of philosophy. And let Phaedrus answer you.

PHAEDRUS: Put the question.

SOCRATES: Is not rhetoric, taken generally, a universal art of enchanting the mind by arguments; which is practised not only in courts and public assemblies, but in private houses also, having to do with all matters, great as well as small, good and bad alike, and is in all equally right, and equally to be esteemed—that is what you have heard?

PHAEDRUS: Nay, not exactly that; I should say rather that I have heard the art confined to speaking and writing in lawsuits, and to speaking in public assemblies—not extended farther.

SOCRATES: Then I suppose that you have only heard of the rhetoric of Nestor and Odysseus, which they composed in their leisure hours when at Troy, and never of the rhetoric of Palamedes?

PHAEDRUS: No more than of Nestor and Odysseus, unless Gorgias is your Nestor, and Thrasymachus or Theodorus your Odysseus.

SOCRATES: Perhaps that is my meaning. But let us leave them. And do you tell me, instead, what are plaintiff and defendant doing in a law court—are they not contending?

PHAEDRUS: Exactly so.

SOCRATES: About the just and unjust—that is the matter in dispute?

PHAEDRUS: Yes.

SOCRATES: And a professor of the art will make the same thing appear to the same persons to be at one time just, at another time, if he is so inclined, to be unjust?

PHAEDRUS: Exactly.

SOCRATES: And when he speaks in the assembly, he will make the same things seem good to the city at one time, and at another time the reverse of good?

PHAEDRUS: That is true.

SOCRATES: Have we not heard of the Eleatic Palamedes (Zeno), who has an art of speaking by which he makes the same things appear to his hearers like and unlike, one and many, at rest and in motion?

PHAEDRUS: Very true.

SOCRATES: The art of disputation, then, is not confined to the courts and the assembly, but is one and the same in every use of language; this is the art, if there be such an art, which is able to find a likeness of everything to which a likeness can be found, and draws into the light of day the likenesses and disguises which are used by others?

PHAEDRUS: How do you mean?

SOCRATES: Let me put the matter thus: When will there be more chance of deception—when the difference is large or small?

PHAEDRUS: When the difference is small.

SOCRATES: And you will be less likely to be discovered in passing by degrees into the other extreme than when you go all at once?

PHAEDRUS: Of course.

SOCRATES: He, then, who would deceive others, and not be deceived, must exactly know the real likenesses and differences of things?

PHAEDRUS: He must.

SOCRATES: And if he is ignorant of the true nature of any subject, how can he detect the greater or less degree of likeness in other things to that of which by the hypothesis he is ignorant?

PHAEDRUS: He cannot.

SOCRATES: And when men are deceived and their notions are at variance with realities, it is clear that the error slips in through resemblances?

PHAEDRUS: Yes, that is the way.

SOCRATES: Then he who would be a master of the art must understand the real nature of everything; or he will never know either how to make the gradual departure from truth into the opposite of truth which is effected by the help of resemblances, or how to avoid it?

PHAEDRUS: He will not.

SOCRATES: He then, who being ignorant of the truth aims at appearances, will only attain an art of rhetoric which is ridiculous and is not an art at all?

PHAEDRUS: That may be expected.

SOCRATES: Shall I propose that we look for examples of art

and want of art, according to our notion of them, in the speech of Lysias which you have in your hand, and in my own speech?

PHAEDRUS: Nothing could be better; and indeed I think that our previous argument has been too abstract and wanting in illustrations.

SOCRATES: Yes; and the two speeches happen to afford a very good example of the way in which the speaker who knows the truth may, without any serious purpose, steal away the hearts of his hearers. This piece of good-fortune I attribute to the local deities; and, perhaps, the prophets of the Muses who are singing over our heads may have imparted their inspiration to me. For I do not imagine that I have any rhetorical art of my own.

PHAEDRUS: Granted; if you will only please to get on.

SOCRATES: Suppose that you read me the first words of Lysias' speech.

PHAEDRUS: 'You know how matters stand with me, and how, as I conceive, they might be arranged for our common interest; and I maintain that I ought not to fail in my suit, because I am not your lover. For lovers repent—'

SOCRATES: Enough:—Now, shall I point out the rhetorical error of those words?

PHAEDRUS: Yes.

SOCRATES: Every one is aware that about some things we are agreed, whereas about other things we differ.

PHAEDRUS: I think that I understand you; but will you explain yourself?

SOCRATES: When any one speaks of iron and silver, is not the same thing present in the minds of all?

PHAEDRUS: Certainly.

SOCRATES: But when any one speaks of justice and goodness we part company and are at odds with one another and with ourselves?

PHAEDRUS: Precisely.

SOCRATES: Then in some things we agree, but not in others?

PHAEDRUS: That is true.

SOCRATES: In which are we more likely to be deceived, and in which has rhetoric the greater power?

PHAEDRUS: Clearly, in the uncertain class.

SOCRATES: Then the rhetorician ought to make a regular division, and acquire a distinct notion of both classes, as well of that in which the many err, as of that in which they do not err?

PHAEDRUS: He who made such a distinction would have an excellent principle.

SOCRATES: Yes; and in the next place he must have a keen eye for the observation of particulars in speaking, and not make a mistake about the class to which they are to be referred.

PHAEDRUS: Certainly.

SOCRATES: Now to which class does love belong—to the debatable or to the undisputed class?

PHAEDRUS: To the debatable, clearly; for if not, do you think that love would have allowed you to say as you did, that he is an evil both to the lover and the beloved, and also the greatest possible good?

SOCRATES: Capital. But will you tell me whether I defined love at the beginning of my speech? for, having been in an ecstasy, I cannot well remember.

PHAEDRUS: Yes, indeed; that you did, and no mistake.

SOCRATES: Then I perceive that the Nymphs of Achelous and Pan the son of Hermes, who inspired me, were far better rhetoricians than Lysias the son of Cephalus. Alas! how inferior to them he is! But perhaps I am mistaken; and Lysias at the commencement of his lover's speech did insist on our supposing love to be something or other which he fancied him to be, and according to this model he fashioned and framed the remainder of his discourse. Suppose we read his beginning over again:

PHAEDRUS: If you please; but you will not find what you want.

SOCRATES: Read, that I may have his exact words.

PHAEDRUS: 'You know how matters stand with me, and how, as I conceive, they might be arranged for our common interest;

and I maintain I ought not to fail in my suit because I am not your lover, for lovers repent of the kindnesses which they have shown, when their love is over.'

SOCRATES: Here he appears to have done just the reverse of what he ought; for he has begun at the end, and is swimming on his back through the flood to the place of starting. His address to the fair youth begins where the lover would have ended. Am I not right, sweet Phaedrus?

PHAEDRUS: Yes, indeed, Socrates; he does begin at the end.

SOCRATES: Then as to the other topics—are they not thrown down anyhow? Is there any principle in them? Why should the next topic follow next in order, or any other topic? I cannot help fancying in my ignorance that he wrote off boldly just what came into his head, but I dare say that you would recognize a rhetorical necessity in the succession of the several parts of the composition?

PHAEDRUS: You have too good an opinion of me if you think that I have any such insight into his principles of composition.

SOCRATES: At any rate, you will allow that every discourse ought to be a living creature, having a body of its own and a head and feet; there should be a middle, beginning, and end, adapted to one another and to the whole?

PHAEDRUS: Certainly.

SOCRATES: Can this be said of the discourse of Lysias? See whether you can find any more connexion in his words than in the epitaph which is said by some to have been inscribed on the grave of Midas the Phrygian.

PHAEDRUS: What is there remarkable in the epitaph?

SOCRATES: It is as follows:—

'I am a maiden of bronze and lie on the tomb of Midas; So long as water flows and tall trees grow, So long here on this spot by his sad tomb abiding, I shall declare to passers-by that Midas sleeps below.'

Now in this rhyme whether a line comes first or comes last, as you will perceive, makes no difference.

PHAEDRUS: You are making fun of that oration of ours.

SOCRATES: Well, I will say no more about your friend's speech lest I should give offence to you; although I think that it might furnish many other examples of what a man ought rather to avoid. But I will proceed to the other speech, which, as I think, is also suggestive to students of rhetoric.

PHAEDRUS: In what way?

SOCRATES: The two speeches, as you may remember, were unlike; the one argued that the lover and the other that the non-lover ought to be accepted.

PHAEDRUS: And right manfully.

SOCRATES: You should rather say 'madly;' and madness was the argument of them, for, as I said, 'love is a madness.'

PHAEDRUS: Yes.

SOCRATES: And of madness there were two kinds; one produced by human infirmity, the other was a divine release of the soul from the yoke of custom and convention.

PHAEDRUS: True.

SOCRATES: The divine madness was subdivided into four kinds, prophetic, initiatory, poetic, erotic, having four gods presiding over them; the first was the inspiration of Apollo, the second that of Dionysus, the third that of the Muses, the fourth that of Aphrodite and Eros. In the description of the last kind of madness, which was also said to be the best, we spoke of the affection of love in a figure, into which we introduced a tolerably credible and possibly true though partly erring myth, which was also a hymn in honour of Love, who is your lord and also mine, Phaedrus, and the guardian of fair children, and to him we sung the hymn in measured and solemn strain.

PHAEDRUS: I know that I had great pleasure in listening to you.

SOCRATES: Let us take this instance and note how the transition was made from blame to praise.

PHAEDRUS: What do you mean?

SOCRATES: I mean to say that the composition was mostly playful. Yet in these chance fancies of the hour were involved two principles of which we should be too glad to have a clearer description if art could give us one.

PHAEDRUS: What are they?

SOCRATES: First, the comprehension of scattered particulars in one idea; as in our definition of love, which whether true or false certainly gave clearness and consistency to the discourse, the speaker should define his several notions and so make his meaning clear.

PHAEDRUS: What is the other principle, Socrates?

SOCRATES: The second principle is that of division into species according to the natural formation, where the joint is, not breaking any part as a bad carver might. Just as our two discourses, alike assumed, first of all, a single form of unreason; and then, as the body which from being one becomes double and may be divided into a left side and right side, each having parts right and left of the same name—after this manner the speaker proceeded to divide the parts of the left side and did not desist until he found in them an evil or left-handed love which he justly reviled; and the other discourse leading us to the madness which lay on the right side, found another love, also having the same name, but divine, which the speaker held up before us and applauded and affirmed to be the author of the greatest benefits.

PHAEDRUS: Most true.

SOCRATES: I am myself a great lover of these processes of division and generalization; they help me to speak and to think. And if I find any man who is able to see 'a One and Many' in nature, him I follow, and 'walk in his footsteps as if he were a god.' And those who have this art, I have hitherto been in the habit of calling dialecticians; but God knows whether the name is right or not. And I should like to know what name you would give to your or to Lysias' disciples, and whether this may not be that famous art of rhetoric which Thrasymachus and others teach and practise? Skilful speakers they are, and impart their skill to any who is willing to make kings of them and to bring gifts to them.

PHAEDRUS: Yes, they are royal men; but their art is not the same with the art of those whom you call, and rightly, in my opinion, dialecticians:—Still we are in the dark about rhetoric.

SOCRATES: What do you mean? The remains of it, if there be anything remaining which can be brought under rules of art, must be a fine thing; and, at any rate, is not to be despised by you and me. But how much is left?

PHAEDRUS: There is a great deal surely to be found in books of rhetoric?

SOCRATES: Yes; thank you for reminding me:—There is the exordium, showing how the speech should begin, if I remember rightly; that is what you mean—the niceties of the art?

PHAEDRUS: Yes.

SOCRATES: Then follows the statement of facts, and upon that witnesses; thirdly, proofs; fourthly, probabilities are to come; the great Byzantian word-maker also speaks, if I am not mistaken, of confirmation and further confirmation.

PHAEDRUS: You mean the excellent Theodorus.

SOCRATES: Yes; and he tells how refutation or further refutation is to be managed, whether in accusation or defence. I ought also to mention the illustrious Parian, Evenus, who first invented insinuations and indirect praises; and also indirect censures, which according to some he put into verse to help the memory. But shall I 'to dumb forgetfulness consign' Tisias and Gorgias, who are not ignorant that probability is superior to truth, and who by force of argument make the little appear great and the great little, disguise the new in old fashions and the old in new fashions, and have discovered forms for everything, either short or going on to infinity. I remember Prodicus laughing when I told him of this; he said that he had himself discovered the true rule of art, which was to be neither long nor short, but of a convenient length.

PHAEDRUS: Well done, Prodicus!

SOCRATES: Then there is Hippias the Elean stranger, who probably agrees with him.

PHAEDRUS: Yes.

SOCRATES: And there is also Polus, who has treasuries of diplasiology, and gnomology, and eikonology, and who teaches in them the names of which Licymnius made him a present; they were to give a polish.

PHAEDRUS: Had not Protagoras something of the same sort?

SOCRATES: Yes, rules of correct diction and many other fine precepts; for the 'sorrows of a poor old man,' or any other pathetic case, no one is better than the Chalcedonian giant; he can put a whole company of people into a passion and out of one again by his mighty magic, and is first-rate at inventing or disposing of any sort of calumny on any grounds or none. All of them agree in asserting that a speech should end in a recapitulation, though they do not all agree to use the same word.

PHAEDRUS: You mean that there should be a summing up of the arguments in order to remind the hearers of them.

SOCRATES: I have now said all that I have to say of the art of rhetoric: have you anything to add?

PHAEDRUS: Not much; nothing very important.

SOCRATES: Leave the unimportant and let us bring the really important question into the light of day, which is: What power has this art of rhetoric, and when?

PHAEDRUS: A very great power in public meetings.

SOCRATES: It has. But I should like to know whether you have the same feeling as I have about the rhetoricians? To me there seem to be a great many holes in their web.

PHAEDRUS: Give an example.

SOCRATES: I will. Suppose a person to come to your friend Eryximachus, or to his father Acumenus, and to say to him: 'I know how to apply drugs which shall have either a heating or a cooling effect, and I can give a vomit and also a purge, and all that sort of thing; and knowing all this, as I do, I claim to be a physician and to make physicians by imparting this knowledge to others,'—what do you suppose that they would say?

PHAEDRUS: They would be sure to ask him whether he knew

'to whom' he would give his medicines, and 'when,' and 'how much.'

SOCRATES: And suppose that he were to reply: 'No; I know nothing of all that; I expect the patient who consults me to be able to do these things for himself'?

PHAEDRUS: They would say in reply that he is a madman or a pedant who fancies that he is a physician because he has read something in a book, or has stumbled on a prescription or two, although he has no real understanding of the art of medicine.

SOCRATES: And suppose a person were to come to Sophocles or Euripides and say that he knows how to make a very long speech about a small matter, and a short speech about a great matter, and also a sorrowful speech, or a terrible, or threatening speech, or any other kind of speech, and in teaching this fancies that he is teaching the art of tragedy—?

PHAEDRUS: They too would surely laugh at him if he fancies that tragedy is anything but the arranging of these elements in a manner which will be suitable to one another and to the whole.

SOCRATES: But I do not suppose that they would be rude or abusive to him: Would they not treat him as a musician a man who thinks that he is a harmonist because he knows how to pitch the highest and lowest note; happening to meet such an one he would not say to him savagely, 'Fool, you are mad!' But like a musician, in a gentle and harmonious tone of voice, he would answer: 'My good friend, he who would be a harmonist must certainly know this, and yet he may understand nothing of harmony if he has not got beyond your stage of knowledge, for you only know the preliminaries of harmony and not harmony itself.'

PHAEDRUS: Very true.

SOCRATES: And will not Sophocles say to the display of the would-be tragedian, that this is not tragedy but the preliminaries of tragedy? and will not Acumenus say the same of medicine to the would-be physician?

PHAEDRUS: Quite true.

SOCRATES: And if Adrastus the mellifluous or Pericles heard of these wonderful arts, brachylogies and eikonologies and all the hard names which we have been endeavouring to draw into the light of day, what would they say? Instead of losing temper and applying uncomplimentary epithets, as you and I have been doing, to the authors of such an imaginary art, their superior wisdom would rather censure us, as well as them. 'Have a little patience, Phaedrus and Socrates, they would say; you should not be in such a passion with those who from some want of dialectical skill are unable to define the nature of rhetoric, and consequently suppose that they have found the art in the preliminary conditions of it, and when these have been taught by them to others, fancy that the whole art of rhetoric has been taught by them; but as to using the several instruments of the art effectively, or making the composition a whole,—an application of it such as this is they regard as an easy thing which their disciples may make for themselves.'

PHAEDRUS: I quite admit, Socrates, that the art of rhetoric which these men teach and of which they write is such as you describe—there I agree with you. But I still want to know where and how the true art of rhetoric and persuasion is to be acquired.

SOCRATES: The perfection which is required of the finished orator is, or rather must be, like the perfection of anything else; partly given by nature, but may also be assisted by art. If you have the natural power and add to it knowledge and practice, you will be a distinguished speaker; if you fall short in either of these, you will be to that extent defective. But the art, as far as there is an art, of rhetoric does not lie in the direction of Lysias or Thrasymachus.

PHAEDRUS: In what direction then?

SOCRATES: I conceive Pericles to have been the most accomplished of rhetoricians.

PHAEDRUS: What of that?

SOCRATES: All the great arts require discussion and high speculation about the truths of nature; hence come loftiness of thought and completeness of execution. And this, as I conceive, was the quality which, in addition to his natural gifts, Pericles acquired from his intercourse with Anaxagoras whom he happened to know. He was thus imbued with the higher philosophy, and attained the knowledge of Mind and the negative of Mind, which were favourite themes of Anaxagoras, and applied what suited his purpose to the art of speaking.

PHAEDRUS: Explain.

SOCRATES: Rhetoric is like medicine.

PHAEDRUS: How so?

SOCRATES: Why, because medicine has to define the nature of the body and rhetoric of the soul—if we would proceed, not empirically but scientifically, in the one case to impart health and strength by giving medicine and food, in the other to implant the conviction or virtue which you desire, by the right application of words and training.

PHAEDRUS: There, Socrates, I suspect that you are right.

SOCRATES: And do you think that you can know the nature of the soul intelligently without knowing the nature of the whole?

PHAEDRUS: Hippocrates the Asclepiad says that the nature even of the body can only be understood as a whole. (Compare Charmides.)

SOCRATES: Yes, friend, and he was right:—still, we ought not to be content with the name of Hippocrates, but to examine and see whether his argument agrees with his conception of nature.

PHAEDRUS: I agree.

SOCRATES: Then consider what truth as well as Hippocrates says about this or about any other nature. Ought we not to consider first whether that which we wish to learn and to teach is a simple or multiform thing, and if simple, then to enquire what power it has of acting or being acted upon in relation to other things, and if multiform, then to number the forms; and see first in the case of one of them, and then in the case of all of them, what is that power of acting or being acted upon which makes each and all of them to be what they are?

PHAEDRUS: You may very likely be right, Socrates.

SOCRATES: The method which proceeds without analysis is like the groping of a blind man. Yet, surely, he who is an artist ought not to admit of a comparison with the blind, or deaf. The rhetorician, who teaches his pupil to speak scientifically, will particularly set forth the nature of that being to which he addresses his speeches; and this, I conceive, to be the soul.

PHAEDRUS: Certainly.

SOCRATES: His whole effort is directed to the soul; for in that he seeks to produce conviction.

PHAEDRUS: Yes.

SOCRATES: Then clearly, Thrasymachus or any one else who teaches rhetoric in earnest will give an exact description of the nature of the soul; which will enable us to see whether she be single and same, or, like the body, multiform. That is what we should call showing the nature of the soul.

PHAEDRUS: Exactly.

SOCRATES: He will explain, secondly, the mode in which she acts or is acted upon.

PHAEDRUS: True.

SOCRATES: Thirdly, having classified men and speeches, and their kinds and affections, and adapted them to one another, he will tell the reasons of his arrangement, and show why one soul is persuaded by a particular form of argument, and another not.

PHAEDRUS: You have hit upon a very good way.

SOCRATES: Yes, that is the true and only way in which any subject can be set forth or treated by rules of art, whether in speaking or writing. But the writers of the present day, at whose feet you have sat, craftily conceal the nature of the soul which they know quite well. Nor, until they adopt our method of reading and writing, can we admit that they write by rules of art?

PHAEDRUS: What is our method?

SOCRATES: I cannot give you the exact details; but I should like to tell you generally, as far as is in my power, how a man ought to proceed according to rules of art.

PHAEDRUS: Let me hear.

SOCRATES: Oratory is the art of enchanting the soul, and therefore he who would be an orator has to learn the differences of human souls—they are so many and of such a nature, and from them come the differences between man and man. Having proceeded thus far in his analysis, he will next divide speeches into their different classes:—'Such and such persons,' he will say, are affected by this or that kind of speech in this or that way,' and he will tell you why. The pupil must have a good theoretical notion of them first, and then he must have experience of them in actual life, and be able to follow them with all his senses about him, or he will never get beyond the precepts of his masters. But when he understands what persons are persuaded by what arguments, and sees the person about whom he was speaking in the abstract actually before him, and knows that it is he, and can say to himself, 'This is the man or this is the character who ought to have a certain argument applied to him in order to convince him of a certain opinion;'—he who knows all this, and knows also when he should speak and when he should refrain, and when he should use pithy sayings, pathetic appeals, sensational effects, and all the other modes of speech which he has learned;—when, I say, he knows the times and seasons of all these things, then, and not till then, he is a perfect master of his art; but if he fail in any of these points, whether in speaking or teaching or writing them, and yet declares that he speaks by rules of art, he who says 'I don't believe you' has the better of him. Well, the teacher will say, is this, Phaedrus and Socrates, your account of the so-called art of rhetoric, or am I to look for another?

PHAEDRUS: He must take this, Socrates, for there is no possibility of another, and yet the creation of such an art is not easy.

SOCRATES: Very true; and therefore let us consider this matter in every light, and see whether we cannot find a shorter and easier road; there is no use in taking a long rough roundabout way if there be a shorter and easier one. And I wish that you would try and remember whether you have heard from Lysias or any one else anything which might be of service to us.

PHAEDRUS: If trying would avail, then I might; but at the moment I can think of nothing.

SOCRATES: Suppose I tell you something which somebody who knows told me.

PHAEDRUS: Certainly.

SOCRATES: May not 'the wolf,' as the proverb says, 'claim a hearing'?

PHAEDRUS: Do you say what can be said for him.

SOCRATES: He will argue that there is no use in putting a solemn face on these matters, or in going round and round, until you arrive at first principles; for, as I said at first, when the question is of justice and good, or is a question in which men are concerned who are just and good, either by nature or habit, he who would be a skilful rhetorician has no need of truth—for that in courts of law men literally care nothing about truth, but only about conviction: and this is based on probability, to which he who would be a skilful orator should therefore give his whole attention. And they say also that there are cases in which the actual facts, if they are improbable, ought to be withheld, and only the probabilities should be told either in accusation or defence, and that always in speaking, the orator should keep probability in view, and say good-bye to the truth. And the observance of this principle throughout a speech furnishes the whole art.

PHAEDRUS: That is what the professors of rhetoric do actually say, Socrates. I have not forgotten that we have quite briefly touched upon this matter already; with them the point is all-important.

SOCRATES: I dare say that you are familiar with Tisias. Does he not define probability to be that which the many think?

PHAEDRUS: Certainly, he does.

SOCRATES: I believe that he has a clever and ingenious case of this sort:—He supposes a feeble and valiant man to have assaulted a strong and cowardly one, and to have robbed him of his coat or of something or other; he is brought into court, and then Tisias says that both parties should tell lies: the coward should say that he was assaulted by more men than one; the other should prove that they were alone, and should argue thus: 'How could a weak man like me have assaulted a strong man like him?' The complainant will not like to confess his own cowardice, and will therefore invent some other lie which his adversary will thus gain an opportunity of refuting. And there are other devices of the same kind which have a place in the system. Am I not right, Phaedrus?

PHAEDRUS: Certainly.

SOCRATES: Bless me, what a wonderfully mysterious art is this which Tisias or some other gentleman, in whatever name or country he rejoices, has discovered. Shall we say a word to him or not?

PHAEDRUS: What shall we say to him?

SOCRATES: Let us tell him that, before he appeared, you and I were saying that the probability of which he speaks was engendered in the minds of the many by the likeness of the truth, and we had just been affirming that he who knew the truth would always know best how to discover the resemblances of the truth. If he has anything else to say about the art of speaking we should like to hear him; but if not, we are satisfied with our own view, that unless a man estimates the various characters of his hearers and is able to divide all things into classes and to comprehend them under single ideas, he will never be a skilful rhetorician even within the limits of human power. And this skill he will not attain without a great deal of trouble, which a good man ought to undergo, not for the sake of speaking and acting before men, but in order that he may be able to say what is acceptable to God and always to act acceptably to Him as far as in him lies; for there is a saying of wiser men than ourselves, that a man of sense should not try to please his fellow-servants (at least this should not be his first object) but his good and noble masters; and therefore if the way is long and circuitous, marvel not at this, for, where the end is great, there we may take the longer road, but not for lesser ends such as yours. Truly, the argument may say, Tisias, that if you do not mind going so far, rhetoric has a fair beginning here.

PHAEDRUS: I think, Socrates, that this is admirable, if only practicable.

SOCRATES: But even to fail in an honourable object is honourable.

PHAEDRUS: True.

SOCRATES: Enough appears to have been said by us of a true and false art of speaking.

PHAEDRUS: Certainly.

SOCRATES: But there is something yet to be said of propriety and impropriety of writing.

PHAEDRUS: Yes.

SOCRATES: Do you know how you can speak or act about rhetoric in a manner which will be acceptable to God?

PHAEDRUS: No, indeed. Do you?

SOCRATES: I have heard a tradition of the ancients, whether true or not they only know; although if we had found the truth ourselves, do you think that we should care much about the opinions of men?

PHAEDRUS: Your question needs no answer; but I wish that you would tell me what you say that you have heard.

SOCRATES: At the Egyptian city of Naucratis, there was a famous old god, whose name was Theuth; the bird which is called the Ibis is sacred to him, and he was the inventor of many arts, such as arithmetic and calculation and geometry and astronomy and draughts and dice, but his great discovery was the use of letters. Now in those days the god Thamus was the king of the whole country of Egypt; and he dwelt in that great city of Upper Egypt which the Hellenes call Egyptian Thebes, and the god himself is called by them Ammon. To him came Theuth and showed his inventions, desiring that the other Egyptians might be allowed to have the benefit of them; he enumerated them, and Thamus enquired about their several uses, and praised some of them and censured others, as he approved or disapproved of them. It would take a long time to repeat all that Thamus said to Theuth in praise or blame of the various arts. But when they came to letters, This, said Theuth, will make the Egyptians wiser and give them better memories; it is a specific both for the memory and for the wit. Thamus replied: O most ingenious Theuth, the parent or inventor of an art is not always the best judge of the utility or inutility of his own inventions to the users of them. And in this instance, you who are the father of letters, from a paternal love of your own children have been led to attribute to them a quality which they cannot have; for this discovery of yours will create forgetfulness in the learners' souls, because they will not use their memories; they will trust to the external written characters and not remember of themselves. The specific which you have discovered is an aid not to memory, but to reminiscence, and you give your disciples not truth, but only the semblance of truth; they will be hearers of many things and will have learned nothing; they will appear to be omniscient and will generally know nothing; they will be tiresome company, having the show of wisdom without the reality.

PHAEDRUS: Yes, Socrates, you can easily invent tales of Egypt, or of any other country.

SOCRATES: There was a tradition in the temple of Dodona that oaks first gave prophetic utterances. The men of old, unlike in their simplicity to young philosophy, deemed that if they heard the truth even from 'oak or rock,' it was enough for them; whereas you seem to consider not whether a thing is or is not true, but who the speaker is and from what country the tale comes.

PHAEDRUS: I acknowledge the justice of your rebuke; and I think that the Theban is right in his view about letters.

SOCRATES: He would be a very simple person, and quite a stranger to the oracles of Thamus or Ammon, who should leave in writing or receive in writing any art under the idea that the written word would be intelligible or certain; or who deemed that writing was at all better than knowledge and recollection of the same matters?

PHAEDRUS: That is most true.

SOCRATES: I cannot help feeling, Phaedrus, that writing is unfortunately like painting; for the creations of the painter have the attitude of life, and yet if you ask them a question they preserve a solemn silence. And the same may be said of speeches. You would imagine that they had intelligence, but if you want to know anything and put a question to one of them, the speaker always gives one unvarying answer. And when they have been once written down they are tumbled about anywhere among those who may or may not understand them, and know not to whom they should reply, to whom not: and, if they are maltreated or abused, they have no parent to protect them; and they cannot protect or defend themselves.

PHAEDRUS: That again is most true.

SOCRATES: Is there not another kind of word or speech far better than this, and having far greater power—a son of the same family, but lawfully begotten?

PHAEDRUS: Whom do you mean, and what is his origin?

SOCRATES: I mean an intelligent word graven in the soul of the learner, which can defend itself, and knows when to speak and when to be silent.

PHAEDRUS: You mean the living word of knowledge which has a soul, and of which the written word is properly no more than an image?

SOCRATES: Yes, of course that is what I mean. And now may I be allowed to ask you a question: Would a husbandman, who is a man of sense, take the seeds, which he values and which he wishes to bear fruit, and in sober seriousness plant them during the heat of summer, in some garden of Adonis, that he may rejoice when he sees them in eight days appearing in beauty? at least he would do so, if at all, only for the sake of amusement and pastime. But when he is in earnest he sows in fitting soil, and practises husbandry, and is satisfied if in eight months the seeds which he has sown arrive at perfection?

PHAEDRUS: Yes, Socrates, that will be his way when he is in earnest; he will do the other, as you say, only in play.

SOCRATES: And can we suppose that he who knows the just and good and honourable has less understanding, than the husbandman, about his own seeds?

PHAEDRUS: Certainly not.

SOCRATES: Then he will not seriously incline to 'write' his thoughts 'in water' with pen and ink, sowing words which can neither speak for themselves nor teach the truth adequately to others?

PHAEDRUS: No, that is not likely.

SOCRATES: No, that is not likely—in the garden of letters he will sow and plant, but only for the sake of recreation and amusement; he will write them down as memorials to be treasured against the forgetfulness of old age, by himself, or by any other old man who is treading the same path. He will rejoice in beholding their tender growth; and while others are refreshing their souls with banqueting and the like, this will be the pastime in which his days are spent.

PHAEDRUS: A pastime, Socrates, as noble as the other is ignoble, the pastime of a man who can be amused by serious talk, and can discourse merrily about justice and the like.

SOCRATES: True, Phaedrus. But nobler far is the serious pursuit of the dialectician, who, finding a congenial soul, by the help of science sows and plants therein words which are able to help themselves and him who planted them, and are not unfruitful, but have in them a seed which others brought up in different soils render immortal, making the possessors of it happy to the utmost extent of human happiness.

PHAEDRUS: Far nobler, certainly.

SOCRATES: And now, Phaedrus, having agreed upon the premises we may decide about the conclusion.

PHAEDRUS: About what conclusion?

SOCRATES: About Lysias, whom we censured, and his art of writing, and his discourses, and the rhetorical skill or want of skill which was shown in them—these are the questions which we sought to determine, and they brought us to this point. And I think that we are now pretty well informed about the nature of art and its opposite.

PHAEDRUS: Yes, I think with you; but I wish that you would repeat what was said.

SOCRATES: Until a man knows the truth of the several particulars of which he is writing or speaking, and is able to define them as they are, and having defined them again to divide them until they can be no longer divided, and until in like manner he is able to discern the nature of the soul, and discover the different modes of discourse which are adapted to different natures, and to arrange and dispose them in such a way that the simple form of speech may be addressed to the simpler nature, and the complex and composite to the more complex nature— until he has accomplished all this, he will be unable to handle arguments according to rules of art, as far as their nature allows them to be subjected to art, either for the purpose of teaching or persuading;—such is the view which is implied in the whole preceding argument.

PHAEDRUS: Yes, that was our view, certainly.

SOCRATES: Secondly, as to the censure which was passed on the speaking or writing of discourses, and how they might be rightly or wrongly censured—did not our previous argument show—?

PHAEDRUS: Show what?

SOCRATES: That whether Lysias or any other writer that ever was or will be, whether private man or statesman, proposes laws and so becomes the author of a political treatise, fancying that there is any great certainty and clearness in his performance, the fact of his so writing is only a disgrace to him, whatever men may say. For not to know the nature of justice and injustice, and good and evil, and not to be able to distinguish the dream from the reality, cannot in truth be otherwise than disgraceful to him, even though he have the applause of the whole world.

PHAEDRUS: Certainly.

SOCRATES: But he who thinks that in the written word there is necessarily much which is not serious, and that neither poetry nor prose, spoken or written, is of any great value, if, like the compositions of the rhapsodes, they are only recited in order to be believed, and not with any view to criticism or instruction; and who thinks that even the best of writings are but a reminiscence of what we know, and that only in principles of justice and goodness and nobility taught and communicated orally for the sake of instruction and graven in the soul, which is the true way of writing, is there clearness and perfection and seriousness, and that such principles are a man's own and his legitimate offspring;— being, in the first place, the word which he finds in his own bosom; secondly, the brethren and descendants and relations of his idea which have been duly implanted by him in the souls of others;—and who cares for them and no others—this is the right sort of man; and you and I, Phaedrus, would pray that we may become like him.

PHAEDRUS: That is most assuredly my desire and prayer.

SOCRATES: And now the play is played out; and of rhetoric enough. Go and tell Lysias that to the fountain and school of the Nymphs we went down, and were bidden by them to convey a message to him and to other composers of speeches—to Homer and other writers of poems, whether set to music or not; and to Solon and others who have composed writings in the form of political discourses which they would term laws—to all of them we are to say that if their compositions are based on knowledge of the truth, and they can defend or prove them, when they are put to the test, by spoken arguments, which leave their writings poor in comparison of them, then they are to be called, not only poets, orators, legislators, but are worthy of a higher name, befitting the serious pursuit of their life.

PHAEDRUS: What name would you assign to them?

SOCRATES: Wise, I may not call them; for that is a great name which belongs to God alone,—lovers of wisdom or philosophers is their modest and befitting title.

PHAEDRUS: Very suitable.

SOCRATES: And he who cannot rise above his own compilations and compositions, which he has been long patching and piecing, adding some and taking away some, may be justly called poet or speech-maker or law-maker.

PHAEDRUS: Certainly.

SOCRATES: Now go and tell this to your companion.

PHAEDRUS: But there is also a friend of yours who ought not to be forgotten.

SOCRATES: Who is he?

PHAEDRUS: Isocrates the fair:—What message will you send to him, and how shall we describe him?

SOCRATES: Isocrates is still young, Phaedrus; but I am willing to hazard a prophecy concerning him.

PHAEDRUS: What would you prophesy?

SOCRATES: I think that he has a genius which soars above the orations of Lysias, and that his character is cast in a finer mould. My impression of him is that he will marvellously improve as he grows older, and that all former rhetoricians will be as children in comparison of him. And I believe that he will not be satisfied with rhetoric, but that there is in him a divine inspiration which will lead him to things higher still. For he has an element of philosophy in his nature. This is the message of the gods dwelling in this place, and which I will myself deliver to Isocrates, who is my delight; and do you give the other to Lysias, who is yours.

PHAEDRUS: I will; and now as the heat is abated let us depart.

SOCRATES: Should we not offer up a prayer first of all to the local deities?

PHAEDRUS: By all means.

SOCRATES: Beloved Pan, and all ye other gods who haunt this place, give me beauty in the inward soul; and may the outward and inward man be at one. May I reckon the wise to be the wealthy, and may I have such a quantity of gold as a temperate man and he only can bear and carry.—Anything more? The prayer, I think, is enough for me.

PHAEDRUS: Ask the same for me, for friends should have all things in common.

SOCRATES: Let us go.

Made in United States
Orlando, FL
24 January 2023

29017331R00064